Filipino Americans

FOOTSTEPS TO

AmericA

Filipino
Americans

by Alexandra Bandon

CONTRA COSTA COUNTY LIBRARY

new
Discovery
B·O·O·K·S

New York

Maxwell Macmillan Canada
Toronto

Maxwell Macmillan International
New York   Oxford   Singapore   Sydney

ACKNOWLEDGMENT

Special thanks to the immigrants who shared their personal stories.
Their names have been change to protect their privacy.

Photo Credits

Front cover: Philippine Department of Tourism
Front and back cover: (flag photo): Richard Bachmann
Filipino American National Historical Society Collection: 11, 14, 34, 42, 59, 65, 70, 77,
93, 96, 98, 101, 107; Frank Mancao: 74
Filipinos: Forgotten Asian Americans by Fred Cordova: 9
UPI/Bettmann: 18, 24, 80
Reuters/Bettmann: 22, 27, 49, 91
The George Bacon Collection, Hawaii State Archives: 40

New Discovery Books
Macmillan Publishing Company
866 Third Avenue
New York, NY 10022

Maxwell Macmillan Canada Inc.
1200 Eglinton Avenue East
Suite 200
Don Mills, Ontario M3C 3N1

Macmillan Publishing Company is part of the Maxwell Communication Group of Companies.

First edition
Printed in the United States of America

10   9   8   7   6   5   4   3   2   1

LIBRARY OF CONGRESS CATALOGING-IN-PUBLICATION DATA
Bandon, Alexandra.
Filipino Americans / Alexandra Bandon. — 1st ed.
p. cm. — (Footsteps to America)
Includes bibliographical references.
Summary: Discusses the reasons for Filipino immigration to the United States and the conditions they have found here, using case studies to describe the lifestyles of Filipino Americans.
ISBN 0-02-768143-2
1. Filipino Americans—Juvenile literature. 2. Filipino Americans—History—Juvenile literature.
[1. Filipino Americans. 2. Philippines—Emigration and immigration. 3. United States—Emigration and immigration.] I. Title II. Series.
E184.F4B36 1993   973'.049921—dc20   92-42205

Contents

Part I
The Land They Left Behind

≡ **1** ≡

Why Do They Leave?

Philippine History

The Philippines is a group of islands located in the Pacific Ocean off the southeast coast of Asia. There are more than 7,100 islands, of which only 400 or so are inhabited. In the Philippines, the men are called Filipinos; the women; Filipinas. More than 87 different languages and dialects are spoken.

The earliest inhabitants of the Philippines were Negritos, who lived on many of the islands of Oceania and in southeastern Asia. Indonesians arrived later, and Asian Muslims settled in the south of the island chain in the 15th century. In 1521, a Portuguese explorer named Fernão de Magalhães, known to us in English as Ferdinand Magellan, was the first European to land on what was eventually called the Philippine Islands. Magellan, who was working for the Spanish King Charles V, was killed six weeks after he landed by a native chief, Lapu Lapu, who refused Spanish rule. Twenty-seven years later, the islands were named Philip for the crown prince (and soon-to-be king) of Spain. From the 1520s onward, the Spanish sent many expeditions to the Philippines, but it took them until 1571 to complete their conquest of the islands. Thus began over 300 years of harsh Spanish colonialism.

During their reign, the Spanish treated the native Filipino

people horribly, denying them all privileges while usurping their natural resources and economy, profiting handsomely. Only the *illustrados,* descendants of the Spanish rulers who were entirely or at least largely European, could be educated, hold office, or control large properties.

Many native Filipino men were taken forcibly into the Spanish navy, or armada, and made to work as slaves. These Filipinos labored on Spanish galleons along the trade routes between the Philippines and the Spanish colony in Mexico. Many of them jumped ship at Acapulco, the chief Spanish port in America, to escape their ruthless overseers. From there they eventually made their way north into the Louisiana Territory, where they and their descendants, known as Manilamen, lived in the bayous and marshes around New Orleans. In the early 20th century, upward of a thousand descendants of the original Manilamen lived in the area. The Manilamen were the first Filipino Americans.

"Filipino American" describes a Filipino who has come to live in the United States permanently. When people leave their native country, they are emigrants; when they arrive in this country, they are immigrants (leaving a country is emigrating; coming to a country is immigrating). The children of Filipino immigrants are second-generation Filipinos. All Filipino Americans are part of the larger group of Asian Americans, which includes immigrants from China, Japan, Korea, Vietnam, and the other Asian countries.

The *Pensionados*

The first large wave of Filipino immigration to the United States did not begin until the turn of the 20th century. In 1898 the Spanish-American War broke out when the United States, which had promised to help the Spanish colony of Cuba win independence, attacked the Spanish fleet in Manila Bay, in the Philippines. Having involved the Philippines in the war, the United States promised to help the Filipinos achieve independence as well. However, when the Treaty of Paris was signed in December 1898, ending the war, the Philippines was given up by the Spanish only to become a colony of the United States.

The Filipinos were stunned, feeling they had been betrayed by the United States. In 1899 they began a bloody rebellion against the U.S. troops, which over the next three years claimed the lives of 200,000 Filipinos, including children and other civilians, as U.S. forces killed anyone suspected of being a rebel.

Some Americans were outraged, too. The war with the Philippines was as controversial in its time as the Vietnam War would be in the 1960s. Noted Americans such as Mark Twain and Andrew Carnegie protested our government's treatment of the Filipino people. Nonetheless, the Filipinos, hopelessly outarmed by the United States, lost their struggle for independence.

A uniformed U.S. soldier in the Philippines contrasts with a traditionally garbed Filipina during the Spanish-American War, 1899. After the war, Filipinos resented the presence of Americans, whom they thought would grant them independence.

Although President William McKinley chose in 1898 to keep the Philippines as a colony, he also recognized the injustice of the United States going back on its word to the Filipinos. He thus decided to set the stage for an eventual, smooth transition toward Philippine independence by establishing government and education systems in the Philippines based on American models. Americans brought to the Philippines health education, curbing the spread of tropical diseases, and built roads, railroads, and bridges. "There was nothing left for us to do but take them all, and to educate the Filipinos, and uplift and civilize and Christianize them," McKinley once told a group of clergymen.

In the early years of the 20th century, the United States also established an excellent school system for the Filipinos, where all were welcome, not just the elite *ilustrados*. American teachers (known as Thomasites because they arrived on a ship named the *St. Thomas*) flocked to the Philippines for the "dangerous task of educating the natives."

From this education system came the first of a great wave of Filipino immigrants to the United States. Between 1903 and 1910, the American government sponsored 500 *pensionados* to come to the United States and study. The *pensionados* were the best Filipino students and were chosen to live with host families in the United States to study at American high schools and universities (Philippine schools provided free education only through the eighth grade). It was expected that the *pensionados* would gain skills and knowledge that could help the Philippines as an independent country. In the United States, the *pensionados* studied government, medicine, and many other subjects that would prove useful to them as the future leaders of their country.

Hawaiian Sugar Plantations

At the same time the *pensionados* were making their mark on American soil, the first of a vast wave of Filipino laborers landed in Honolulu, Hawaii. These Filipinos, members of the Ilocano community, an agricultural tribe, were recruited by the Hawaiian Sugar Planters Association (HSPA) to cut sugarcane in the Hawaiian territory. The HSPA needed the Filipinos because the Chinese and Japanese laborers the association had been importing had been forbidden to immigrate by new U.S. laws. The Ilocano needed the work because their own territory was overpopulated and their land was no longer fertile. The HSPA promised the Ilocano free passage to Hawaii, housing, and food.

At first the Ilocano had not been easily convinced by the recruiters. An initial recruitment program had been abandoned when the Ilocano showed no interest. Subsequently, the HSPA tried everything: The group held lectures and showed films that made Hawaii look like a dreamland. The organization promised great prosperity to the Filipinos and glossed over the grueling realities of work in the cane fields. Despite the HSPA's efforts, only 15 Ilocano came to Hawaii on the association's first sponsored boat, instead of the 300 Ilocano that had been hoped for.

But when the Ilocano laborers in Hawaii wrote home about their experiences, they told of pleasant conditions on the sugar plantations and sent money in every letter. Those who returned to their native land came dressed in fashionable, well-made suits and had made enough money to live as rich men in the Philippines. In an underdeveloped land with no cars, bad roads, few horses, and only the most primitive intersettlement communications, the newly affluent sugar-plantation workers looked like visiting kings. Soon, many Filipinos wanted to go to Hawaii and get a share of the riches to be had there. By 1926, the HSPA no longer had to recruit. In fact, they had to turn workers away.

Though the HSPA had originally hoped to transport whole Ilocano villages to Hawaii to demonstrate the ease with which the Filipinos could adjust to plantation life, the Philippine women refused to go. They felt that traveling to Hawaii and living on the plantations was not respectable. They were also worried that Catholicism, which was the primary faith of the Filipino people,

was not well enough established in Hawaii. By 1920, the ratio in
Hawaii of Filipino men to Filipino women was about twenty to one.

The Filipinos Go to the Mainland

Hawaii was only one place to which Filipinos traveled look-ing for work. The men returning to the Philippines from Hawaii with stories of wealth inspired many others to try their hands at working on the American mainland. Hopeful Filipinos looking for work as agricultural laborers boarded ships in Manila headed for San Francisco and Seattle.

Between 1907 and 1930, about 50,000 Filipinos arrived on the mainland. Many came to work in agriculture, but others jour-neyed to the continental United States to attend high schools and universities. Stories brought back to the Philippines by the *pensionados* had inspired thousands of Filipinos to emigrate in order to continue their education. Intending to study during the day and work at night (as many had done in the Philippines), Filipino students readily invested in the $70 ship fare to the United States. Many families mortgaged their homes in hope that the money they gave to their children to go to the United States for an education would be repaid a thousandfold upon their return.

World War II

Through the 1920s and 1930s, Filipinos continued to leave their homes for the wealth of opportunities in the United States.

(continued on page 18)

Gabriel De León
A Picture from Home

Gabriel de León lives in Honolulu, Hawaii. He is of Filipino descent and is married to an Irish-American woman. He and his wife own a resort hotel.

I remember my grandfather's stories. He was one of the first of the Ilocano to come to Hawaii and work in the sugarcane fields. He needed the work, and was glad to get it. The money was good for the time—that was 1910—and he was able to send some back home. But he was a young man, and there were no Filipino women in Hawaii. He was lonely, and it was hard for the men to meet women.

When my grandfather was forty, a man in his *compang* [a plantation-worker "family"] showed him a photograph of his sister. She was very pretty; my grandfather said he fell in love with her right away. Her name was Elena. I've seen that picture countless times. She was wearing a pretty flowered dress. Grandfather said he liked her smile.

At first, my grandfather sent messages through the letters of Elena's brother. "Tell your sister Elena that if she likes flowers, she would love the flowers here"—things like that. She would send messages back. Then they began to write to each other directly. They wrote for two years. The funny thing is that for all that time, my grandfather wouldn't send Elena his picture. He was too afraid that she wouldn't think him handsome, or that she would think he was too old.

They met under sad circumstances. The brother died, and Elena and her father came to Hawaii to bury him. My grandfather met them at the boat. When he saw Elena in person, he thought she was too beautiful to ever want him. He stood by and admired her, but was afraid to court her.

Elena and her father decided to stay in Hawaii, since they had no family left in the Philippines. My grandfather became a friend of the family. But he didn't try to win Elena's hand. He didn't believe that she would want him as a husband. He treated her with great respect, naturally, but he never said a word about love or marriage.

Finally, after a few months, Elena cooked my grandfather a big dinner and then told him she was moving to the mainland. She wasn't, really. She had just gotten tired of waiting. Well, that did it. My grandfather finally asked Elena to marry him, and she said yes (although she also said that why she'd want a man with a head like a rock, she didn't know). Years later, every time my grandmother would tell me that part of the story, she would look over at my grandfather and laugh. After forty years, she was still teasing him.

They had six children, including my father. When my grandfather died, five years ago, he left me enough money to start my business. He didn't want me to have to work in the fields as he and my father did. My grandfather was a good man.

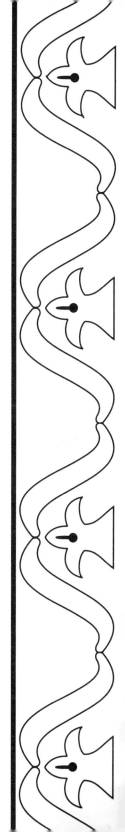

A U.S. soldier issues American uniforms, food, and munitions to Filipino guerillas in 1944. During the Japanese occupation of the Philippines during World War II, the Philippine army became part of the U.S. military.

But then, on December 8, 1941, just a day after they had bombed Pearl Harbor, Hawaii, the Japanese attacked the Philippines. All emigration from the Philippines was cut off abruptly.

U.S. troops stationed in the Philippines joined forces with Filipino troops to fight off the Japanese and, later, to lead a strong resistance movement during the Japanese occupation of the Philippines. General Douglas McArthur commanded the United States Armed Forces of the Far East (USAFFE), into which the

entire Philippine Army and many Philippine nurses were inducted.
Both Philippine and American soldiers endured the notorious
Bataan Death March, in which 70,000 Allied soldiers were forced
by the Japanese to march to concentration camps. Almost 20,000
died on the march, most of them Filipinos.

When the war was over, the Philippines was a devastated
country. Filipinos had years of rebuilding ahead of them. The task
of starting over seemed too overwhelming for some citizens. For
many, the jobs and homes they had before the war were gone com-
pletely, and the pain of staying where there were only sad memories was too much to bear. Leaving the country may have been the
only hope they had of taking care of their families.

Many of the Filipinos who emigrated immediately after World
War II were veterans of the forces that had fought the Japanese.
By virtue of their induction into the United States Army, they were
eligible to become U.S. citizens. They took this opportunity to
leave behind unpleasant memories and follow their dreams to the
United States.

Many Filipinas, too, had worked for the resistance during the
war. They had spied for McArthur during the Japanese occupation,
delivered messages to U.S. and Philippine resistance forces, and
cared for the wounded. Many met American men and fell in love
with them. Dating between Filipinas and American servicemen was
common, in fact, and gave rise to the phrase *"hanggang pier,"* which
means "until the pier only" (referring to the belief that romances
between Filipinas and Americans would last only until the
Americans shipped out.) Despite skepticism, though, many Filipinas
married American men and became war brides, leaving behind the
Philippines for a new life with their husbands in the United States.

Post-World War II Emigration

After World War II, emigration from the Philippines to the United States continued, but at a lower rate. In 1934 the Tydings-McDuffie Act had made the Philippines a Commonwealth (a related but essentially self-governing territory) of the United States. The act also mandated that precisely ten years from its passage the Philippines would be totally independent. (Independence was delayed by the Japanese occupation during World War II and was not officially declared until July 4, 1946.) Unfortunately for the Filipinos, the act established a quota (a limit) of 100 Filipino immigrants per year. Because the quota for the Philippines was so low, few Filipinos could travel to America to become permanent residents.

The postwar Filipino immigrants were very different from the agricultural laborers who had come before the war. These new immigrants were educated professionals seeking better opportunities outside the Philippines. Many had been trained in the Philippines to be doctors, lawyers, nurses, engineers, or teachers, but finding the working conditions unbearable in their own country, they fled to the United States looking for better career opportunities.

When President Lyndon Johnson signed the Immigration and Nationality Act of 1965, the 100-person annual quota for the Philippines became an annual quota of 20,000; Filipinos headed to the United States in droves. Most of these emigrants were, as were their immediate predecessors, professionals, seeking further training in their specialties and higher salaries.

From World War II to the present, the atmosphere in which

Filipino professionals work in their own country has declined
steadily. At first, many professionals left the Philippines because
there was a surplus of well-educated people there: They had
become doctors or lawyers only to find upon graduation that there
were no jobs for them. In the war-ravaged Philippines, only engineers and contractors needed to help rebuild the country were in
high demand. Most of the other educated Filipinos found themselves forced to take their skills outside the country.

In the later decades, Filipinos continued to find it difficult to
benefit from the years and money spent on their education.
Currently, practical training is limited in many fields, and though
professionals make a lot of money by Philippine standards, their
salaries often do not compensate for the initial outlay of time and
money invested in their education. Furthermore, government support in many fields is limited: Scientists are not funded for
research, nor are their projects taken seriously by either the government or the universities, unless the work is seen as having
immediate practical benefit to the country. The Philippines' economy cannot support scientists who work for the sake of learning.
The constant monitoring of scientists' work by the government,
which desires only discoveries that might aid the failing Filipino
economy, interferes with research to the point that scientists are
driven to emigrate and seek work elsewhere.

The result of this mass departure of intellectuals and professionals has been labeled by some as a brain drain. In fact, *one-half*
of the physicians trained in the Philippines emigrate each year,
leaving behind enormous deficiencies in the domestic medical
field. Similar percentages of nurses, engineers, and teachers
depart as well. Many scientists mockingly refer to their predica-
ment in the Philippines as brain rot, the result of not being able to

teach or research in their own fields. University professors are often forced to teach classes that have nothing to do with their field of expertise simply because there are no funds for classes in the subjects they do know.

The brain drain, however, has one advantage for the Philippines. The money that emigrating professionals earn abroad is often sent back to support their families. As U.S. salaries can be as much as ten to twenty times higher than Philippine salaries for comparable work, and as goods and services in the Philippines often cost only a sixth of what they might in the United States, the Philippine economy is greatly boosted by the imported funds. Yet the practice of sending money back to

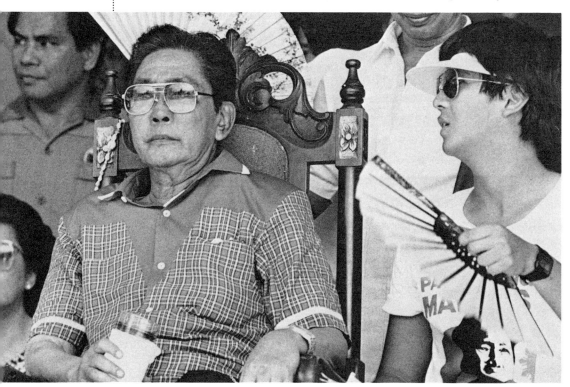

the Philippines is part of a vicious cycle, for that money is most often used to educate family members who in turn leave the Philippines for better opportunities abroad.

The Political Climate

Along with economic reasons for emigrating, many Filipinos cite political unrest as the motivation for their departure. Since independence, Philippine politics has been plagued by corruption, favoritism, and violence. Despite many attempts by past and present presidents to ensure human rights, violations still prevail. Since the 1940s, opposing political parties in the Philippines have been known to threaten and even kill one another's candidates and members, though this sort of behavior did not become commonplace until Ferdinand E. Marcos became president in 1965.

Ferdinand Marcos's political career rose from the ashes of World War II. Exploiting his reputation as a member of the Philippine resistance during the Japanese occupation, Marcos first made headlines when, as a law student during the waning period of American colonial rule, he successfully defended himself against charges that he had killed his father's political opponent. Later, he became a flamboyant attorney and was widely admired. He was elected president of the Philippines in 1965; in 1972 he declared martial law, ending the democracy established almost 75 years earlier under American colonial rule (martial law places the military, instead of the civilian government and the police, in control of a country). In order to maintain his power, Marcos rewrote the Philippine Constitution so that he could serve more than two terms in office. During the next 14 years, Marcos was charged

Soldiers with drawn guns stand beside the body of slain Filipino opposition leader Benigno Aquino (foreground) in 1983. Most Filipinos assumed President Ferdinand Marcos was responsible for ordering Aquino's murder.

repeatedly by his opponents with corruption, rigging elections, military abuses, and *nepotism* (the practice of granting favors from a high office to friends and relatives).

Marcos's tenure as president saw the economic decline of the Philippines and the establishment of political fear and paranoia. Local elections were fraught with violence, often instigated by Marcos's overpowerful military. Each year after Marcos's election saw an increase in election-related deaths.

At first, ironically, Marcos claimed to be a reformer and promised the Filipino people a redistribution of land and wealth. Yet most of the land he seized and the industries he nationalized ended up in his or his friends' hands. Nothing was done to ease the plight of the poor. When Marcos was elected, the Philippines was the richest country in Southeast Asia; by the end of his reign, it was one of the poorest. He ignored the industrial and agricultural needs of his country while creating an enormous debt.

Many Filipinos emigrated under Marcos's reign, when they could. Two noteworthy emigrants during the 1970s were Benigno and Corazon Aquino. Benigno Aquino had been one of Marcos's chief political opponents and had been thrown into jail for his work against martial law. When the Aquinos emigrated to the United States, Marcos warned Benigno Aquino that he would be arrested if he ever returned to Philippine soil. In 1983, Benigno Aquino did attempt to return, believing the political situation in his country had improved. He was shot dead as he stepped off the airplane in Manila. It was widely assumed that the order for the assassination had come from Marcos, though no one was able to prove it. The accusation was a terrible blow to Marcos's political career and in 1986 he was deposed by Corazon Aquino, Benigno's widow, after a hotly contested election.

The election of Corazon Aquino promised many changes in the Philippines. She declared a human-rights policy designed to end the abuses that had existed under her predecessor. Attempting to heal the depressed economic situation, she courted foreign industry to invest in the Philippines. Yet her success in aiding her country and stemming the mass exodus of her fellow citizens was limited.

Despite the valiant efforts of the Aquino government, the Philippine economy did not recover. A population boom, magnified by long-standing laws against contraception and abortion, has led to the highest unemployment rate in the Philippines since World War II. Three quarters of a million people enter the work force each year with little hope of finding jobs. Unemployment leads inevitably to poverty; nearly half of all Filipino deaths are caused by malnutrition, and two thirds of the country's urban poor have no running water, sewage systems, or garbage pickup. And many Filipinos continue to take jobs outside the country—not just in the United States, but in Hong Kong as maids or in the Middle East as workers on oil rigs—because the pay is so much better there.

Furthermore, the unsteady political climate in the Philippines has scared away foreign investment. The country's Communist party and its New People's Army (NPA) gained supporters during Marcos's rule and remained strong after Aquino's election, even threatening her overthrow. Aquino authorized the Philippine military to attempt to control the NPA, and vigilante groups originating in the army led the fight. Many people died and continue to die in the battle between the New People's Army and the Philippine Army. Human-rights monitors fled the country for fear of being murdered. A Filipino lawyer now living in New York

Rebels in the New People's Army preparing an attack. The NPA, part of the Communist party in the Philippines, emerged in the 1970s and 1980s, in reaction to Ferdinand Marcos's military rule.

explained that Filipinos emigrated under Marcos to avoid jail but left under Aquino to avoid death. Amnesty International, an organization that monitors human-rights violations around the world, commended the Aquino government for releasing Marcos's political prisoners and for asserting a progressive policy on human rights, but it also condemned the violations committed by the government and the army-sponsored vigilante groups.

In May 1992, Aquino stepped aside after a single term as president, endorsing her defense minister, Fidel V. Ramos, as the presidential candidate of choice against such opponents as Miriam Defensor Santiago (who won many Filipinos over by campaigning against government corruption and insensitivity to the poor) and Imelda Marcos, the widow of Ferdinand Marcos. After an election labeled the freest in the Philippines in over 20 years (though Santiago and many of the other candidates charged election fraud against Ramos) and a month of deliberations over the final vote count, Fidel Ramos was affirmed as president by the Philippine Congress.

Ramos, a West Point graduate who had been a key figure in the Marcos regime but who went on to lead the 1986 coup that put Corazon Aquino in power, has proposed peace negotiations with both the NPA and the vigilante groups. He is also the first Protestant president of the Philippines, and may therefore approach the population-control issue in a much different manner than did the Roman Catholic Aquino. Clearly, Ramos has the potential to improve the political and economic climate in the Philippines during his six-year term and to slow down the Filipino exodus.

Alan Zobel
Political Exiles

Alan Zobel was a Manila newspaperman who protested the Marcos regime and was forced to leave his country in 1979. He is now a freelance journalist living in New York City.

I left because I had to. My wife was threatened as well as myself. It wasn't easy at first. I drove a cab for five years. I tried to write articles, but all I knew was Philippine politics, and nobody cared about that then. My wife got a job as a maid in a hotel.

My wife and I were watching the news when we saw that Benigno Aquino had been assassinated. Together, we wept.

After that, there was a flurry of interest in Philippine politics, and I got some work as a researcher on a news magazine. That led to a writing job. I was pretty settled in New York when Corazon Aquino was elected, and my wife and I discussed whether we should go back. We decided to stay because things were so uncertain there, and because my wife had just entered a university.

My friends in the Philippines who were going to leave but stayed because of Aquino are now talking about coming to New York. They are full of grief and anger about what's happening there. But they stay.

What greets us if we return? The country that we love, yes. But my wife is now in law school. In a year, she'll graduate. I write about politics and human rights, important issues that need to be examined. I don't want to write the truth and have to look over my shoulder. I don't want to worry about what could happen to my wife and child because of what I do. I have come to love and appreciate the American respect for freedom. So we stay.

✳   ✳   ✳

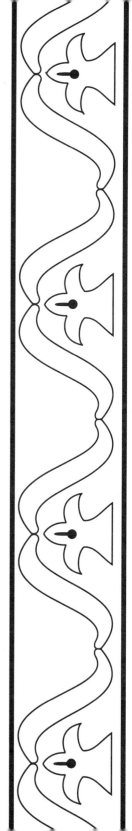

≡ 2 ≡

Why the United States?

The Influence of the United States During Colonial Rule

It cannot be denied that the 48 years that the United States held the Philippines as a colony greatly influenced the Filipino people. One of the three most common languages of the Philippines is English (the other two are Tagalog, the national language; and Spanish). The Constitution of the Philippines, mandating a presidency, a Congress, and a Supreme Court, is based entirely on the U.S. system. Culturally speaking, American fashions and fads have always made their way to the Philippines quickly, and Filipino singers often copy the musical style of famous American entertainers.

The "Americanization" of the Philippines began after the Spanish-American War, when the United States took a country oppressed by the Spanish for more than three centuries and made it its only major colony, turning it into a functioning democracy in which the rights of the people were respected. Stanley Karnow, author of *In Our Image: America's Empire in the Philippines,* wrote in a *New York Times* article, "Curiously, most Filipinos forgave and forgot [the broken promise of independence]. Even the original nationalist leaders eventually swore allegiance to America—

which, as if to atone for its cruelty, ruled the Philippines with unusual benevolence for a half a century."

Americans established free public schools, teaching the Filipinos a common language that would help unite them as a country. They brought in medical technology, vaccinating against smallpox and other deadly diseases. And by supporting universal education, they established the means by which future generations of Filipinos could learn this technology for themselves.

They also brought with them stories of life in the United States. Freedom, wealth, and opportunity were in every description the Thomasites provided for their Filipino students. How, then, could the Filipinos resist coming to the United States to see if they could live like the much-admired Americans? As citizens of a U.S. colony, Filipinos were U.S. nationals and traveled with U.S. passports, so they felt American. Even now, more than four decades since their independence, Filipinos explain that they feel a certain kinship with the United States.

The Unique Opportunities in the United States

Each group of Filipinos who voyaged to the United States came for a different reason. The *pensionados* came to gain knowledge available only in American universities, knowledge that would be helpful to their country when they returned. (And, as was mentioned before, many *pensionados* remained in the United States after their education was over.) For the agricultural workers in Hawaii, the motivation was purely economical. The salaries offered by the

HSPA meant that many of the workers could not only support their families back in the Philippines, but could also buy them property and houses that had previously been out of reach.

Both of these early groups were drawn to the United States by specific programs. If the *pensionado* program had not existed or the HSPA had not needed laborers, many of the Filipinos who immigrated to this country might never have left their homeland in the first place. Still, after these first workers paved the way, thousands more came to the United States with no encouragement from recruiters or government scholarships.

Most of the Filipinos who came to the United States mainland in the early years of Filipino immigration were laborers who took jobs in agriculture, in salmon canneries, or in domestic service in hotels and restaurants or as house servants. Most never intended to stay in the United States forever; they expected to amass a fortune and return to the Philippines as rich men (they *were* mostly men). Many worked hard in the United States and did succeed in getting an education and earning those riches, but there were others who found less then they expected. Because pride prohibited them from returning home as "failures," they stayed in the United States and took low-paying, jobs just to make ends meet, all the while writing home stories of prosperity, so as not to disappoint their friends and families. As success stories, both real and fabricated, made their way back to the Philippines, more Filipinos were encouraged to go to the United States to make their fortunes.

The New Wave of Immigration

During World War II, the Filipino men who fought alongside the Americans in the Philippines took an oath of allegiance to the

United States, as if they were enlisted in the United States Army itself. In 1942, President Franklin Roosevelt signed an act allowing the men who had served in the Philippine Army or in the Philippine Scouts to be naturalized as U.S. citizens before the Philippines reached full independence in 1946. Though the application process did not actually begin until after the Japanese were driven out of the Philippines in 1945, many Filipinos took advantage of the law between 1945 and 1946 to become U.S. citizens.

Some Filipinos didn't just fight alongside the Americans; they enlisted in the United States Navy. As Filipinos were considered American nationals, they were allowed to enlist; after three years of active duty, they could become full-fledged citizens of the United States. In fact, before Philippine independence, a navy hitch was the only way a Filipino could become eligible for U.S. citizenship. Even after Philippine independence, though, Filipinos continued to be allowed to join the United States Navy as part of the two countries' agreement to maintain U.S. military bases on the Philippine Islands.

At the same time, the United States Army formed the First Filipino Infantry Regiment, made up exclusively of Filipinos who had arrived in the United States in previous decades (American troops were racially segregated until after World War II). These infantrymen received automatic citizenship when they took the military oath.

World War II was also the cause of the emigration of the largest group to leave the Philippines between 1945 and 1965. The "war brides" of the native-born American servicemen and the recently naturalized Filipino soldiers came to the United States in droves. Apart from being examined by American agents to see whether they were physically and mentally fit to come to the United States (war brides all over the world were being scrutinized in this manner), the wives and fiancées of servicemen were

A formal gathering of Filipina war brides in 1955.

allowed by the War Brides Act of 1945 to bypass any visa requirements and immigration quotas in place for their countries. Between 1945 and 1965, 118,000 Filipinas took advantage of this act to join their husbands in the United States.

Later, when the United States realized that it had a shortage of "persons with needed skills" who could help the country win the Cold War against communism, the government recruited foreign scientists, technicians, and other skilled workers to keep America ahead in the space program and in other scientific research. As many Filipinos were well educated according to the American system, many emigrated at this time under an encouraging 1952 immigration act.

In 1956 the U.S. government established the Foreign Exchange Visitor Program to induce foreign medical personnel to work in this country, where there was at the time a shortage of doctors and nurses. In return these foreign doctors and nurses supposedly were going to enhance their education at America's top schools. While they primarily found themselves working rather than studying, many of the Filipinos who took advantage of this program changed their temporary visas to permanent visas and stayed in the United States as immigrants. However, the program was limited, and it was not until the passage of the Immigration and Nationality Act of 1965 that medical personnel began immigrating in high numbers.

Post-1965 Immigration

The Immigration and Nationality Act of 1965 greatly relaxed the restrictive quotas on immigration from Asian countries. Before 1965, a country's quota was set as a percentage of the number of people from that country who had lived in the United States in 1890. Now all countries in the Eastern Hemisphere had the same quota: 20,000 immigrants a year. The new law provided numerically equal immigration from all countries while also establishing a system by which potential immigrants were ranked in order of desirability. The most desirable immigrants, aside from immediate relatives of American citizens and permanent residents, were those with special skills much needed in the United States. In the late 1960s and early 1970s, there was a severe shortage of medical workers in this country. Thus Congress deemed doctors, nurses, and medical technicians to be among the most desirable immigrants.

(continued on page 39)

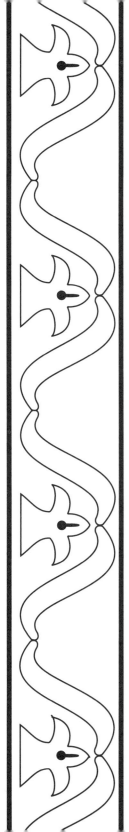

Lea Albor Greenaway
War Bride

Lea Albor Greenaway is a retired nurse living in New York City. She came to the United States as a war bride in 1947.

During the war, I worked at a hospital in Manila. Just after I completed my training, the Japanese occupied the Philippines. It was a very fast introduction to death and suffering.

Someone approached me about working for the resistance, and I liked the idea. My brother had joined the Philippine Army, and by working for the resistance I figured I'd be helping him as well as my country. Several other nurses joined, too, probably more than I knew. If we found out something about troop movements or planes, we would pass along the message. Compared to what some people did, I guess it sounds pretty tame. But if we had been caught, we surely would have been shot.

The Americans didn't retake Manila until 1945, and toward the end, the fighting was bad. The noise of the bombing was constant, and the cots of wounded men spilled out into the hospital corridors. But for me, the worst moment was when I learned what had happened to my brother. He was killed on the Bataan Death March.

A few years ago, there was a show on television about it. I really wanted to watch—I thought enough time had passed. But when I saw how those men looked, I couldn't face it: Skeletons with eyes like black holes. I still pray that my brother died early on, before he had suffered too much. I still pray for him today.

During the war, I also met my husband, Danny. After the Americans retook he Philippines, the soldiers were everywhere. I had a terrific hat, a black straw hat with red roses. A cousin had sent it over from America before the war. Most of my dresses were patched and faded, but I had that hat. I don't think Danny would have noticed me without it. (He doesn't agree, though).

I was so taken with him. He had kind eyes and a mustache . . . and his grin—well, it could blot out the war and the suffering I saw every day. He was from Brooklyn, and that sounded exotic and exciting to me. He talked about hot dogs and the Yankees. Brooklyn seemed very far away, and yet it sounded like a place we could visit together.

All my friends warned me not to expect Danny to marry me. They told me to be happy and enjoy what I had but not to count on anything else. Even when Danny asked me to marry him, they thought it would never happen. But I knew better.

We married in Manila, and Danny was shipped out a week later. I didn't know where. I got a few letters, once in a while, and then nothing. Then came the battle of Iwo Jima. Oh, those days were terrible. We kept hearing about the Allied losses. Over four thousand marines were killed in that one battle, you know. I was frantic. Then one day I met a buddy of Danny's in the hospital. He told me that he had seen Danny only three days before and that he was fine. I'll never forget that day. I stood in the middle of the ward with tears streaming down my face.

I thought everything would be paradise when the war ended. Of course, I was naive. I didn't realize what would happen when I came to the United States as a bride. People were very cruel. A man with an Asian wife was unusual then. And some people thought I was Japanese. Sometimes, while I was waiting for the bus with my husband, people yelled awful things out of cars.

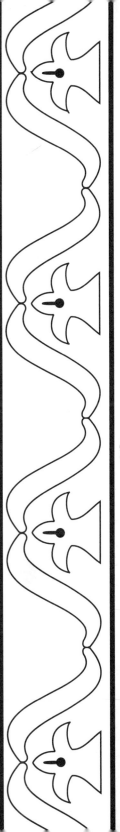

At times, Danny's friends were even worse than the strangers were. Often, when Danny introduced me to a friend, a strange look came over the friend's face. It would make Danny so furious. Even though I was a professional, a head nurse, some people looked at me like I was a concubine. Others saw me as the enemy. Danny soon learned to tell people that his wife was a Filipina. If it still bothered them, he just didn't see them anymore.

So we did encounter some prejudice. But I have not a single regret. Danny went to medical school on the G.I. Bill and became a doctor. Our life together has been busy and full of good things. We have three grown children now. Tomás is a doctor, Angelique is a professor, and Will is a physicist. And now Danny and I are enjoying our free time together. He still likes the Yankees. But I won't let him eat too many hot dogs.

For Filipinos, the change in the yearly quota from 100 immi-grants to 20,000 immigrants was an unprecedented boon, and they took full advantage of the new law. Many well-trained doctors emerged from Philippine schools and went straight to the United States to fill the need for medical personnel. Nurses were being recruited at such a fast rate that many new nursing schools opened in the Philippines purely under the assumption that jobs would exist for their graduates in the United States. Many Filipinos studied nursing and midwifery just to qualify for U.S. immigration.

Even today, Filipinos pursuing the medical professions come to America for training, many with the hope of returning to the Philippines, perhaps after retirement, better able to serve their fellow citizens (though recent licensing restrictions and an end to the doctor shortage in this country have decreased the number of foreign doctors making the trip).

Medical professionals are not the only educated people being drawn to the United States for career reasons. Scientists, such as chemists, psychologists, biologists, and other research-oriented professionals, come to the United States for its scholarly opportunities. Because funds for their studies are not readily available in the Philippines, these scientists find U.S. companies and universities, with their large research grants, to be a great source of support for their work.

Of course, it must be noted that scholarly opportunities aside, American salaries are generally much higher than those in the Philippines. Nurses, for instance, often make two to three times more in this country than they would in the Philippines, and salaries in other professions can be as much as ten to twenty times higher in the United States. In addition, the money Filipinos can save from a few years of labor in the United States often provides a comfortable

Filipino Americans cutting sugar cane in Hawaii, 1953.

existence for many years when they return to the Philippines.

Many blue-collar workers are also taking advantage of the expanded quotas by heading to the United States to work in agriculture or in the tourist industry. The Ilocano who had been recruited by the HSPA in the 1910s organized labor unions over the years and won benefits and high pay from the plantation owners. By the 1950s, the Hawaiian sugar-plantation workers were the highest-paid agricultural workers in the world. Many Ilocano continue to come to Hawaii to work on the plantations and are welcomed by the long-established Ilocano communities there.

═ 3 ═

What Is Their Journey Like?

Crossing the Pacific

nduring the ocean journey from Manila to Honolulu was no easy task for the first Filipino immigrants. Almost invariably, the passengers on these trips were seasick for almost the whole journey. They traveled in steerage quarters, with four to six people cramped into a smelly, dank cabin. Many arrived on American soil having contracted during the voyage dreaded and often deadly diseases such as tuberculosis or spinal meningitis. But the struggle to cross the Pacific Ocean did not start with the walk up the gangplank. Even before that, Filipinos were faced with manipulative recruiters and swindling con men.

When emigrating to the United States became popular in the Philippines, con men made their way to Manila to take advantage of the situation. They convinced unsuspecting would-be émigrés to put up their life's savings for passage on a ship. Then these phony recruiters took off with the money, destroying the lives of the Filipinos who had trusted them.

Even when the recruiters were legitimate, the Filipinos could still be victimized by lies. Faced with a barrage of stories about golden opportunities abroad, Filipino families often mortgaged everything they owned to help their children emigrate to study in the United States. Little did these families realize that once in the United States, their children would be nearly crippled by a lack of funds and, unable to continue their studies, would be forced to work in menial jobs just to make ends meet and, if

Two Filipinas meet an American on a boat to the United States, 1931. Filipinos often paid their life's savings for the cost of a steamship ticket to San Francisco or Seattle.

they were lucky, make enough money to pay off their family's debts.

Upon arriving in this country, many Filipinos were overwhelmed by how unlike the United States was to what they'd been told. They considered themselves equal to native-born Americans, but soon found that they were not only discriminated against because they were Asian, but were considered the lowest sort of Asians, below the Chinese, Japanese, and Koreans. The Filipinos soon learned to depend on one another to survive. It was not uncommon to see an apartment shared by, for instance, five Filipinos, two of whom worked and supported their three roommates who were in school. These groups replaced the large, close-knit families the Filipinos had left behind. Their members helped one another adjust to the American life-style even as they helped one another pay for rent and food.

American Nationals, Not Citizens

One of the biggest obstacles Filipinos faced between 1906 and 1934 was their lack of actual citizenship status in the United States. Filipinos were considered American nationals, which meant that they traveled under American passports, yet they had no rights as citizens and were even ineligible to *become* citizens. (Asians were excluded from naturalization because of a provision in the U.S. Naturalization Act of 1790 that limited citizenship to "free white persons" [blacks were allowed to become citizens in 1870]. This law remained in effect until the Nationality Act of 1946 declared that Asians who had met the eligibility requirements and were permanent residents could become citizens.)

The situation was very complicated for the Filipinos. No person could be considered for naturalization (the process of becoming a citizen) unless that person was first an alien—that is, a foreigner. But because Filipinos were American nationals, they were ineligible for naturalization. Filipinos (except for those serving in the United States military) were trapped in a citizenship limbo.

Filipinos may still join the United States Navy, but Filipino sailors who are not yet citizens have no rights as Americans. Their families have no status as permanent residents, even if they live on American soil in American military bases. If the Filipino in the navy is killed, his or her family can be deported. Still, each year, 24,000 Filipinos take the test to join the navy.

The Tydings-McDuffie Act of 1934

Before 1934, Filipinos could come to the United States in unlimited numbers. But the passage of the Tydings-McDuffie Act, which began the process toward Philippine independence, also established a quota on the number of Filipinos who could immigrate to the United States. Filipinos were now deemed aliens subject to the Immigration Act of 1924, which stated that the annual immigration quota for any foreign country was set at 2 percent of the number of that country's citizens living in the United States at the time of the 1890 census. The act was designed to severely limit immigration from Asia and Eastern Europe while promoting it from Northern Europe. For Filipinos, who had not come to America in any great numbers before 1898, the annual quota was set at the minimum number of 50 (the quota would be raised to 100 in 1946).

On the one hand, this quota was absurdly small and the new law regressively changed the status of Filipinos already living in the United States from American nationals carrying American passports to aliens. On the other hand, for the first time, Filipinos residing in this country were eligible for U.S. citizenship.

The War Years

Even those Filipinos who were entitled to U.S. citizenship during World War II faced obstacles. Because of the Japanese occupation, no Immigration and Naturalization Service (INS) representatives could be sent to accept applications until 1945. And soon after the INS's arrival, President Manuel Roxas of the Philippines asked the new American president, Harry S Truman, to withdraw the representatives because he feared a severe manpower drain on his country. The Philippines desperately needed the help of all its citizens for the massive rebuilding the country faced.   An INS official did return briefly in 1946, but many Filipinos were no longer eligible because they were no longer on active duty. Later that year, the Philippines achieved independence, and the citizenship offer expired. In the end, the many eligible Filipinos had had only a few months to apply for American citizenship; many missed the opportunity altogether.

Obtaining a Visa

The biggest problem for Filipinos who wanted to come to the United States after World War II was the long wait for immigrant visas. The first document an immigrant needs when traveling to the United States is a visa. A visa lets immigration officials know that the government has approved a person's entry into the country. Visas are acquired at the U.S. embassy in the native country of the would-be visitor before he or she travels to the United States.

Immigrant visas are for those intending to stay permanently in the United States. A nonimmigrant visa is issued to those people who want to come to the United States temporarily, and who must identify the reason they are coming (for example, to perform in a concert, to train with the American branch of their company, to attend school, or just to travel as a tourist). Nonimmigrant visitors must usually leave this country or renew their visas within a year (sooner if they are tourists), and their activities in the United States are restricted by the terms of their visa. A visitor with a tourist visa cannot work at all, a student can only go to school, and a concert performer can perform only at the concerts specified to the INS. If a visitor overstays a nonimmigrant visa, he or she is deemed to be in the United States illegally and can be deported.

Any person trying to get a visa to come to the United States, whether it be an immigrant visa or a nonimmigrant visa, must

bring to the U.S. consulate (a local office of the embassy) in his or her country: a birth certificate, a letter from the local police saying that he or she is not a criminal, and a valid passport. All prospective visitors must also submit to a physical to prove they have no contagious diseases. People trying to get what are called family-preference visas must be directly related to an American citizen or to an immigrant who has a permanent-resident card (commonly called a green card).

The Immigration and Nationality Act of 1965

With the passage of the Immigration and Nationality Act of 1965, the wait for visas was relieved, and all persons trying to get visas were now ranked according to to work-related desirability and family ties in the United States. For example, an artist or scientist with "extraordinary" ability and international recognition would be granted a higher priority than an immigrant with only "exceptional" ability. In the interest of uniting families, however, a parent, child, or spouse of a permanent resident of the United States would get absolute first preference and would not be subject to any quotas.

Filipino medical personnel were particularly preferred under this system, especially during the shortages in the 1960s and 1970s. The families of the immigrant agricultural workers of the 1920s and 1930s were now also able to gain easy access to this country. And, of course, immediate relatives of Filipino World War II veterans and war brides came to the United States with no quota restrictions whatsoever.

Yet most of those immigrants who came after 1965 were the privileged of the Philippines. The Philippine economy declined steadily after World War II, and the disparity between rich and poor broadened. During and after the tenure of President Marcos, poverty in the Philippines was rampant. But the poor, the people most affected by the failing economy, had no way to leave, lacking both the funds and the required skills to gain them a favorable rank in the new preference system. To accept poor people with no marketable skills and no relatives on whom to depend would have subjected the United States to the risk of even more people on the welfare rolls.

In spite of this, the poorer Filipinos have found their way to the United States. Some spend everything they have to buy forged passports and visas. Others legally obtain tourist visas, then over-stay their allotted time here. It is estimated that as many as 45,000 Filipinos annually, or 15 to 20 percent of all Filipino tourists, remain in this country after their tourist visas have expired.

Whether they come on fake passports or stay past the expiration of their tourist visas, these Filipinos are then illegals or undocumented immigrants. (In truth, though they *are* in this country illegally, undocumented immigrants are among the most law-abiding people in the United States, committing proportionately fewer crimes here than do U.S. citizens. This may be because they fear arrest and deportation.)

In 1986, Congress passed an immigration act that granted amnesty to any undocumented immigrants living in the United States at the time. Amnesty is the government's way of excusing the illegal entry of undocumented immigrants and legitimizing

A woman sporting a Corazon Aquino T-shirt searches for saleable items in a dump in Manila. The failing economy in the Philippines has left many poor people unable to emigrate to a better life.

them by giving them visas. Those undocumented immigrants who could prove that they had been living in America for five uninterrupted years were given permanent resident status. To the thousands of Filipinos here illegally in 1986 (as well as to all undocumented immigrants), this amnesty was a blessing. No longer did they have to go by fake names and hide their status from their American friends. They could leave this country to visit relatives back home without worrying about how they would get back in, they could obtain jobs without the fear that an employer would discover a phony Social Security number, and they could send for the families they had left behind in the Philippines to join them.

Changes in 1990

Included in the Immigration Act of 1990 was a provision further designed to reunite the families of immigrants who had received amnesty in 1986. While there were revised quotas in place for those desiring employment-based visas or (for the first time) family-based visas, there was now a separate quota established for the relatives of amnesty recipients. Any person related to an amnesty recipient was considered for immigration eligibility apart from all other visa applicants. By enacting this law, Congress intended to curb illegal immigration by legalizing all undocumented workers and their families. Despite the existence of this law, though, illegal immigration has not subsided.

The 1990 act made other adjustments to the rules governing immigration. Congress rearranged the preference system so that even more professionals and artists with "extraordinary abilities" would be welcome, and it tripled the yearly quota for these immigrants. However, while increasing the number of especially skilled people allowed into the United States, the 1990 act also decreased the number of people who could immigrate on family-sponsored visas. Still, because the Philippines has an education system that makes professional training widely available, the ability of Filipinos to acquire employment-based visas is equal to or better than that of people from many other countries.

The Veterans Get Their Day

One group of potential immigrants who benefited immensely from the 1990 act was the World War II veterans who had missed the opportunity to take advantage of the 1942-1946 citizenship. For years, Filipino veterans who had fought alongside Americans during the war had also fought a battle, in the United States courts, to become American citizens. They argued that they had been cheated of the chance to apply for citizenship when President Truman recalled the INS officials in 1945. For years, some of these veterans, who had made their way to the United States illegally, fought deportation as they took their cases to higher and higher courts. Finally, the Supreme Court ruled that those Filipino World War II veterans who could prove that they had tried to make application for citizenship before the 1946 deadline were still eligible.

The 1990 act went further, though, including a provision stating that *any* Filipino who had been eligible to become a U.S. citizen according to the 1942 law could apply for citizenship in a two-year period beginning November 29, 1990. Those desiring citizenship had only to prove that they had been on active-duty status in the USAFFE, the Philippine Army, or the Philippine Scouts during the war. They didn't have to live in the United States to apply, but they were required to demonstrate that they could speak and read English and were knowledgeable concerning U. S. government and history.

Some estimates said that as many as 150,000 Filipino veterans stood to benefit from the 1990 act. Others said the number was lower because many of these Filipinos had died in the Bataan Death March or in the postwar years. According to any estimate, though, Congress quickly realized that the United States would soon be taking in tens of thousands of additional World War II veterans, all of whom were past the age of retirement. To control the financial burden on the government, Congress mandated that these new citizens would not be eligible for any veterans' benefits, such as retirement pay, death pay to families, or health insurance. Despite this significant reduction in the value of their citizenship, many of the Filipino veterans applied instantly, because they saw the benefits they could bring to their families. As American citizens, they could sponsor their spouses and children for immigrant visas, who in turn could sponsor *their* spouses, children, and siblings.

Becoming a Citizen

An immigrant who arrives in the United States is not automatically guaranteed a permanent place here, even if he or she has an immigrant visa. There are many steps to becoming a permanent resident and even more to becoming a citizen. Obtaining a visa is only the first requirement and a Filipino American may have to wait more than seven years after coming to the United States before he or she becomes a citizen.

Immigrants with visas may apply for a green card. Green cards are available to immigrants who are sponsored by their families or who have permanent jobs in the United States. (Because many work visas are for temporary jobs, immigrants with work visas who wish to stay in this country must first obtain a permanent work visa.) Green cards are available to permanent residents six months to a year after they get to the United States, and immigrants with green cards must carry them at all times and report once a year to the Immigration and Naturalization Service.

Shown here are just some of the many forms an alien must complete to get a U.S. visa or U.S. citizenship.

Filipinos wanting to become U.S. citizens must fulfill the same requirements as other countries' emigrants. They must have lived in the United States for over five years or be married to a United States citizen and have lived here three years (some immigrants marry American citizens they don't know just to gain citizenship, but this is illegal and could get the immigrant deported). Would-be citizens must be over 18 and be able to speak, read, and write English at a set level of fluency, though immigrants over 50 years old who have lived in the United States for more than 20 years may be exempted from this requirement. Applicants must also pass a test on basic American history and government.

Before immigrants take this test, however, they must fill out forms to apply for citizenship. The forms are long and complicated, and sometimes immigrants need help completing them. After the forms are submitted to the INS, an applicant may wait six months to two years before he or she is contacted to attend a preliminary hearing, where an oral test is administered and suitability for citizenship is determined.

When the immigrant passes the test, a petition for naturalization is filed on his or her behalf. Within a few months, the immigrant will be contacted to attend a final hearing at which time he or she at last is sworn in as a citizen. Citizenship candidates take an oath of loyalty to the United States, saying that they will support and defend the Constitution (this pledge is much like the oath the president takes!). As citizens, these people can vote, take jobs that require citizenship, and bring their relatives into the country more easily. They also no longer have to carry a green card or notify the INS of their whereabouts, and they can obtain an

American passport—one of the most desirable documents in the world. In other words, they enjoy all the privileges of native-born U.S. citizens.

Where Filipino Americans Live

Like many other immigrant groups, Filipinos are comforted by the nearby presence of fellow immigrants from their country. However, Filipinos usually do not form close-knit Filipino communities in particular areas of towns and cities. They are more likely to follow a job than to follow an ethnic community.

The first Filipino immigrants settled in only a handful of states. Because thousands of Filipino workers went to Hawaii to work on the sugar plantations and to California to work in agriculture, these states have the highest populations of Filipino Americans. Filipinos are one of the largest ethnic minorities in Hawaii and are the single largest Asian group in California (as well as in the whole United States). More than one million Filipino Americans live in Los Angeles alone.

Agricultural workers and salmon canners found work in Washington State and in Alaska in the 1920s and 1930s, while Filipinos settled in San Francisco and Seattle simply because that was where the ships from Manila first landed. The *pensionados* and other students chose cities such as Chicago and Los Angeles, where they attended universities or agricultural colleges, often while working as domestics or on hotel staffs.

Currently, many Filipino Americans opt to live in urban areas where their professional skills are most needed. Only recently have they made their way to the East Coast in significant numbers, but now New York City and its surrounding areas are home to many Filipino Americans. California, Hawaii, Illinois, New York, New Jersey, Washington, Virginia, Texas, Florida, and Pennsylvania boast the largest populations of Filipino Americans, no doubt because these states contain the biggest U.S. cities. Only 7.5 percent of Filipino Americans live in rural areas.

Part II

In the United States

Prejudice and Opportunity

Working Conditions

When Filipinos began emigrating to the United States around the turn of the century, they had visions of a free and equal existence among Americans who had no prejudices. In reality, though, the life that many Filipinos faced upon arriving in this country was hard. For the sugar-plantation workers in Hawaii, working conditions and the living quarters were actually rather good: They were housed by their employers in army-style barracks, well fed, and paid decent wages. But for those who ventured to California or the other West Coast states, no easy living was guaranteed. These immigrants worked mostly in stoop labor, the kind of agricultural work that requires a lot of standing and bending to low crops. Many Filipinos tended asparagus, one of the hardest crops to harvest because its stalks are low to the ground and very difficult to cut. Strong but short people were best suited for this job.

But it wasn't necessarily the work that made life so difficult for the Filipino immigrants. It was the manner in which they were treated by the farm owners. Like many of the minority workers of the 1910s and 1920s, the Filipinos in the rural areas of the West

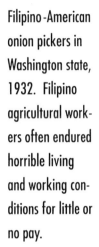

Filipino-American onion pickers in Washington state, 1932. Filipino agricultural workers often endured horrible living and working conditions for little or no pay.

Coast were often crowded into cramped living quarters and given inedible food, conditions that scarcely lived up to the "free room and board" the farmers had promised. The wages were horrible, as well, often as low as 60 cents a day. And many workers were conned into signing contracts that allowed the farmers to deduct exorbitant amounts of money for food and housing.

In his book, *I Have Lived with the American People*, Manuel Buaken tells of his brother, who signed a four-month contract to work on a farm for which he was to be paid $50 per month at the end of the job. For a job that was supposed to provide living quarters and food, this $50 was a good wage. But at the end of the four months, Buaken's brother and the other 14 workers on the farm discovered to their horror that they had overlooked a provision in their contracts that allowed the farmer to deduct from their wages as much as had been spent on their keep. Even though the workers had been housed in a shack with no sanitary facilities and had been fed only rice and beans for the entire four months, their employer claimed expenses that left the Filipinos with a total of $50 to divide among 15 men. Instead of $200, each man made $3.33 for four months of work!

This story is typical of the treatment Filipinos endured as they struggled to find jobs in America in the 1920s. Filipinos who worked in the salmon canneries of Washington and Alaska (called *Alaskeros*) faced the same kinds of working conditions as the farm laborers. Often, the cannery contracts required that a worker buy a suit from the company store, the cost of which would be deducted from his wages. The suit was not even necessary for the job; it was just an excuse for the cannery owners to cheat their workers by overcharging them for something that was virtually worthless. Workers who refused to buy the suit were passed over for the jobs; there were many men willing to take their places.

In the canneries, the working conditions were often poor, and Filipinos usually were given the most menial jobs. Living quarters were cramped and unsanitary, and wages were withheld for inflated cost-of-living expenses. Again, deceptive contracts denied many Filipinos the full wages they earned.

In addition to the maltreatment they suffered at the hands of their employers, Filipinos were often discriminated against by the people living around them. Filipinos were called "little brown

(continued on page 64)

Augusto Rivera
Leaving the Cannery

Augusto Rivera came to the United States in the 1930s. He lives in Seattle, Washington, with his friend Manuel Luz, whom he met on the boat coming over. They have been friends for 50 years.

I got off the boat in Seattle. It was summer, but it was freezing. I had never felt so cold. The fog was so thick you couldn't see more than a foot ahead of you.

My friend Manuel and I weren't worried. We had good jobs lined up at a salmon cannery. We even had a place to live—the company had arranged everything. We were very naive, Manuel and I. Well, we were young. We could take anything.

First of all, they made us buy a suit. No money, they said, don't worry, it will come out of your pay. What could we do, go back home? So we agreed. Then we saw where we were going to be living. A tiny room with five other men. We had to share a bathroom and a shower in the hall with the rest of the men on our floor. The place was filthy and smelled of fish. We looked at each other. This couldn't be, we said. They promised us a nice place. There must be some mistake. But this was it.

At least the wages were good. And the work, well, it was bad, gutting cold fish for hours and hours until you couldn't feel your fingers. At night, you'd lie in bed, and your fingers would throb. You couldn't make a fist. But we kept telling each other it could have been worse, and we had to take what came.

On our days off, we'd walk around the city. We found out that we should stay out of certain neighborhoods. We accepted that, too. I think in those days I was

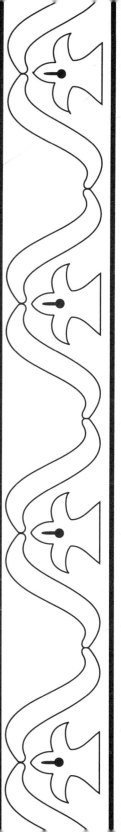

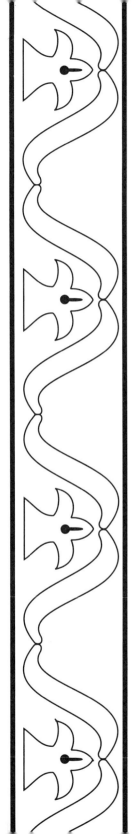

more concerned about how cold I was all the time. I didn't pay attention to prejudice. I didn't let it bother me. I just kept telling myself that after the summer I'd have plenty of money to make a fresh start somewhere else.

Well, after the summer we found out that the company had cheated us. They were charging us for things like towels and soap and never told us. Not only that, but we hardly ever got fresh towels and soap. But no, they said that such things were freshly stocked every week. Plus the suit was expensive, and the room charge was more than they said. But there was no place to go to complain. In the end, we had hardly any money.

Even with all that, some of the men stayed on. It was the Depression, and they were glad to have jobs. But I was a more adventurous type, and I talked Manuel into going south with me. I was restless, and besides, I wanted to get warm. I figured that with farm work, at least I'd work up a sweat.

Well, farm work wasn't much better. In fact, it was worse. We were asparagus workers or did whatever else was available. But conditions were terrible, and prejudice was even worse in the California valleys. One night, Manuel and I went to a dance hall, and a white man picked a fight with some Filipinos next to us. Of course we jumped in to help. Another stupid move. Manuel was stabbed in the arm. We stayed in the south until he got better. But as soon as he recovered, we headed back to Seattle. At least we knew some people there, Manuel said. And he didn't mind the rain and cold. I wasn't convinced, but I went.

There, luck finally found us. There was a letter waiting for Manuel. His mother wrote that a guy from his hometown had a job at the post office. Go see him, his mother said. He has offered to look out for you. Manuel went, and the guy said he'd help him. He would tell Manuel how to become a citizen and he would find a job for him. So in the meanwhile, I found a job as a busboy and Manuel found some part-time gardening work. We waited. There were nights we didn't have enough money for food, but we weren't about to leave Seattle when a good job might come along. I was itching to try Los Angeles this time, but Manuel talked me into staying, so I did. You see, we didn't have family. We didn't have wives. We just had each other.

Finally, Manuel's friend came through. He sent Manuel over to the railroad, and Manuel got a good job there. Eventually, we studied and became American citizens, and Manuel's friend got me a job in the post office. Now that was a good job. I got to look at the letters, the destinations. That could make me sad, because I thought I'd never get to see places like New Mexico or New York City. But do you know what? I have.

Every time I saw the name of a city or town that made me feel restless, made me want to go somewhere, I'd write it down. I collected a list of about fifty cities and towns. I've been to twenty-five of them. This summer, I'm going to Amelia Island in Georgia. I thought it sounded pretty. One thing I know. It will be warm.

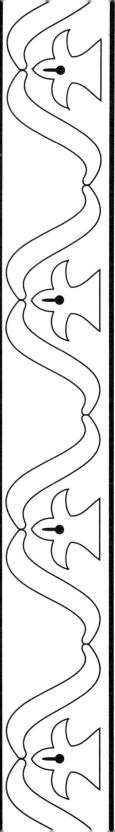

monkeys," and were prohibited from entering stores or restaurants by signs saying: NO DOGS OR FILIPINOS ALLOWED. They were stereotyped as hot-blooded fighters who were interested only in gambling and women. They were denied jobs freely given to less-educated and less-skilled Europeans simply because of the way they looked. They were considered by bigoted whites to be the lowest ethnic group among the already discriminated-against Asians.

The Students

Filipino students faced different obstacles. Though they, too, encountered prejudice, their most difficult struggle was to finish their studies and make enough money to live on. Of the original 500 *pensionados*, only 200 finished their studies and returned to the Philippines to hold positions of importance. Some 14,000 other Filipino students came to this country without government sponsorship between 1910 and 1938, and many of them, too, found it extremely difficult to keep up their studies while making enough money to pay for tuition, room, and board. The Depression of the 1930s stranded many of the students, and rather than go back to the Philippines as "failures," they took the jobs that other, less-privileged Filipinos had been accepting all along: farm workers, dishwashers, busboys, and houseboys. The few who did remain in school worked mornings and nights as domestic servants and studied during the day. During the 1920s and 1930s, it was considered fashionable among whites on the West Coast to hire these Filipino "schoolboys" (though it was even more fashionable to have a Chinese houseboy).

For Filipinos in the United States who were unemployed during the Depression because the few jobs available usually went to whites, there were two hopes for work: In the 1920s, the U.S. Post Office had set aside jobs specifically for Filipinos, and those who held those jobs when the Depression began kept them, and found that their wages, which did not change, bought more as prices plummeted. Filipinos could also find jobs with the Pullman Palace Car Company, which employed most of the porters on passenger trains. Among Filipinos, porter positions were considered very good work, and many took advantage of the opportunity. Those who were lucky enough to have jobs with the post office or with Pullman when times were bad also did their best to support other Filipinos who lived with them or came to them for help.

An *Alaskero* working the line in Sunny Point, Alaska. Filipino Americans were recruited in the 1920s and 1930s to work summers canning salmon.

The Anti-Filipino Movements

Filipinos in California and Washington faced much discrimination in the 1920s and 1930s. They were American nationals, yet they were considered outsiders. During the Depression, when jobs were scarce, Filipinos were among the last to be hired and the first to be fired. Yet prejudiced whites believed that the Filipinos took jobs away from American citizens, and they looked down on them as a rowdy, trouble-causing bunch. In truth, the Filipinos usually took jobs that whites would have refused because the work was "beneath them." Yet local newspapers and public officials still railed against Filipinos as being decadent and dangerous.

The Filipino men who came to the United States in the early part of this century also ran into trouble because of the absence here of Filipino women. In the 1920s, the ratio of Filipino men to Filipino women in the United States was fourteen to one, and most of the Filipinas who were here were either very young or married. Many Filipino men were lonely and longed for companionship. In Hawaii, the men formed *compangs,* small groups of workers that substituted for families. There was always a father figure and several "sons" in each *compang.* For the men in California, however, there were no such *compangs.* Instead, the California Filipinos flocked to dance halls, where they bought ten-cent tickets used to buy dances with the girls (called "taxi dancers") who worked there.

Most of these women were white, and self-appointed "moralists" were offended by the association between Filipino men and white women. They noted that the Filipinos spent much of their free time enjoying cockfights (where brutally trained roosters pecked each other to death while observers wagered on the outcome) and betting in the local gambling houses. They scornfully pointed out that Filipino men often wasted a full week's wages in a single night at these establishments. In truth, Filipinos *did* frequent the dance halls, the gambling houses, and the cockfighting arenas, but it must be acknowledged that they had no other forms of peaceful recreation or entertainment available to them. They had no families to go home to (apart from the absence of Filipino women in this country, many states forbade marriage between Filipinos and whites). They were barred from most restaurants and movie houses.

In October 1929, a riot broke out between whites and Filipinos in the small farming community of Exeter in California's San Joaquin Valley. The fighting started when a Filipino man who was dating a white woman stabbed one of the white men who had been harassing Filipinos at a local carnival. A white mob marched to the local Filipino labor camp, ordered all the residents out, and burned down the housing complex. The local newspapers said the riot was caused by the "natural violent nature" of the Filipinos.

Soon, racist editorials appeared in the newspapers of other farm communities where Filipinos lived and worked. Tensions between Filipinos and whites were blamed exclusively on the Filipinos, and *any* interracial fight was labeled a "racial incident." The Filipino-American papers were slow to respond, mainly because they had always been social-news reporters, not political commentators. In December 1929, when a paper in Watsonville, California, reported that a Filipino dance hall was opening in nearby Palm Beach, the local chamber of commerce passed a resolution unanimously condemning Filipinos as a health and social menace. Then Justice of the Peace D. W. Rohrback published a scathing editorial against Filipinos, denouncing them as violent and primitive and stating that they were "ten years removed from the bolo and the breechcloth."

Within a week, whites were picketing in Watsonville against the Palm Beach dance hall, and brawls were erupting between them and the Filipinos. The papers promptly reported that the Filipinos were marching and rioting. In response, 400 whites attacked the Northern Monterey Filipino Club, injuring many Filipinos. Later that night, a Filipino farm laborer named Fermin Tabera was gunned down in his bunk by machine-gun fire. The rioting continued for five days, while 1,000 Filipinos marched in Los Angeles to protest Tabera's death. In the Philippines, a "Day of Humiliation" was declared to protest both Tabera's death and the local authorities' handling of the riots.

Riots less severe than those in Exeter and Watsonville occurred in the West throughout this period: in Yakima, Washington, in 1928; in Salinas, California, in 1934; and in Lake County, California, in 1939.

In the midst of the uproar, many U.S. politicians believed the problem could be solved by passing laws to bar Filipinos from entering the United States. The first such attempt had actually been made as early as 1928, when a bill was introduced in the House of Representatives that would have excluded Filipinos from immigration to this country altogether. That bill did not, however, make it to the House floor.

Filipino-American newspapers responded to the insults of American whites by demanding independence for the Philippines. Ironically, many of the same U.S. lawmakers who supported legislation to exclude Filipinos from this country *also* wanted Philippine independence, largely because independence would immediately categorize Filipinos residing in this country as aliens subject to restrictive immigration quotas.

Yet independence was not enough to satisfy the exclusionists. Just before the independence act passed, Congress approved the Dickstein Resolution, which provided for repatriation of Filipinos, all expenses paid (repatriation is the act of returning immigrants to their native country), and ensured that no repatriated Filipino could return to the United States without being subject to the new immigration laws. Though the Philippine Society of California also promoted repatriation, only 2,190 Filipinos (out of a possible 45,200) took advantage of the offer.

Discrimination against Filipinos did not always take place in the form of riots and repatriation. In 1922, Salvador Roldan, a Filipino, and his fiancée, a white woman, challenged a miscegenation law (a law forbidding interracial marriages) in California. In *Roldan v. Los Angeles County*, Roldan argued that he and his bride-to-be had had their rights violated when they were refused a marriage license based on a law that stated, "No license must be issued authorizing the marriage of a white person with a Negro, Mulatto, or Mongolian." Rather than challenge the law as racist and unfair, Roldan simply argued that Filipinos were not Mongolians (Chinese), but actually Malays. And though Roldan won his case and was married, the law was quickly changed to read, "No license must be issued authorizing the marriage of a white person with a Negro, Mulatto, Mongolian, or member of the Malay race." Filipinos who wanted to marry whites were forced to go to other states, and their marriages were not recognized in

California or the other U.S. states with similar laws on their books. All miscegenation laws were declared unconstitutional in 1948.

As blue-collar workers, Filipino Americans faced work-related discrimination until the 1930s and 1940s, when they were finally allowed to unionize or join existing unions. At last, Filipino Americans were able to win concessions from employers and end some of the mistreatment they had been subjected to for decades.

A Filipino-American man and his Caucasian wife in the 1930s. Mixed-race marriages, though common, were illegal in many states until 1948 and the cause of much controversy for Filipino Americans.

When the Hawaiian sugar-plantation laborers unionized, they lobbied for higher wages and successfully argued for benefits and better working conditions. By the 1950s, these laborers had become the best-paid agricultural workers in the world!

A Change of Heart

After the Americans and Filipinos joined forces in World War II, Americans' attitudes toward Filipinos changed, giving the Filipinos a new chance. Those Filipinos who were able to get the American citizenship offered to World War II veterans now had the chance to get an education through the GI Bill. Many of these soldiers had been in the United States for years and had faced the brutal discrimination of the Depression years. Now they saw a change of heart in the American people and a new chance to achieve the American dream for which they had emigrated from their home.

For the war brides from the Philippines, coming to the United States was a chance to escape a ravaged country and live like the Americans they admired from afar. Most of the brides adapted to American life easily because they had experienced so much of our culture before and during the war. Before the war, many Filipina had declined to follow the men emigrants to the United States because it was not deemed "respectable." But the presence in their country during the war years of American and Filipino-American soldiers brought about new attitudes among Filipino families. They relaxed many of their strict rules forbidding their daughters to date American men. When the war was over, and many Filipinas left to join their new husbands, other Filipinas

(continued on page 74)

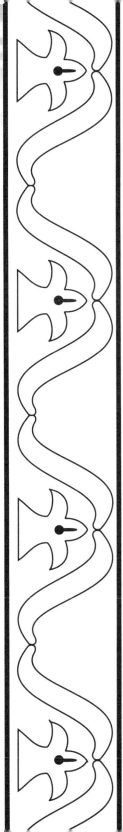

Robert Casal
The Next Generation

Dr. Robert Casal is a Filipino American living in San Francisco, California. He is 42, and he and his wife, who is also a doctor, have two young children.

My wife's family is Italian American, so my children are half-Filipino. The other day my oldest, Kim, asked me where the Philippines were. I showed her on the map. She asked me whether I was born there, and I told her that no, her great-grandfather was. It was the first time my children have asked me any questions about their Filipino heritage. And I am ashamed to say it was the first time I told them how the Casals came to this country. I chose to leave out many of the sad details. Prejudice is an ugly thing to have to tell your children about. But there were some things I wanted them to know.

There was a time, I told my children, when it would have been against the law for me to marry their mother. There was a time when a Filipino could not go to certain restaurants or stores. Even when they spoke English fluently and even when they were well educated, they were barred from certain jobs.

I like that there was incomprehension in my children's eyes. I'm glad that today they don't understand this sort of discrimination. But I want them to know what came before. And their questions got me thinking about my grandfather's stories.

He was an agricultural worker in California in the thirties. He couldn't join a union at that time, so like most Filipino men he took backbreaking work that no one else wanted. But he was determined to make it. He had left the Philippines to make

ood in the United States. He was unusual among Filipino workers in America in that e was married and had a son. Most of the men he worked alongside were single. My grandfather was determined to make it out of the fields. He was trying to save enough money to open a store.

He was living in the San Joaquin Valley during the riots, only a few miles rom Watsonville. He told me stories of how no Filipino felt safe. My grandfather was ot a big man, or a violent man. He just tried to stay out of everyone's way. He told f going out to work in the fields, wondering if someone would take a potshot at him. uckily, my grandfather was well liked by the whites in the community. I think it was robably because he presented no threat. He was married to a Filipina and had chil-dren. He wasn't about to riot.

But tensions were high in the valley, and there were people who saw every ilipino man as an enemy. My grandfather rented a tiny house from the foreman of he farm where he worked. One night, someone set fire to it. Luckily, my grandfa-her woke in time to get his wife and son out. But everything they had was destroyed.

Things didn't really get better until the war. By then, my father was eigh-een, so he enlisted and was sent overseas. He was wounded in the South Pacific and ent home to mend. He was about to be sent back again when the war ended.

Now I look at my daughters and wonder how I can connect them to their her-tage. My family is assimilated. We don't follow many Filipino customs. There is more han just years separating me from my grandfather's life. There is a whole different ulture, a whole different way of looking at things. I can't quite imagine it, but I want ny daughters to know it.

Filipinos proudly marching in a California Fourth of July parade, 1943. During World War II, Americans looked favorably upon Filipinos, their allies in the Pacific.

looked to the United States as a new adventure. They came to this country on family-sponsored visas, as students, or on fiancée visas, and they no longer believed that emigrating alone wasn't respectable.

Filipino Professionals

Many white Americans' revised opinion of Filipinos did not mean that these immigrants no longer encountered challenges in their new home. The educated Filipinos who emigrated to America after the war and after the Immigration and Nationality Act of 1965 faced many obstacles, most of them career-oriented. At first, when the McCarran-Walter Act of 1952 recruited professionals to work in the United States, Filipinos found that their credentials were welcome here. However, as soon as the professional shortages were eliminated, many Filipinos trying to find work in this country stumbled over obstacles in licensing and accreditation.

Each state government controls the rules for licensing its own doctors, lawyers, and other professionals. In California, for example, graduates of foreign schools cannot take the state's licensing exam to become optometrists. Not only optometrists were affected; strict recertification standards affected accountants, doctors, lawyers, architects, and engineers.

Of course, American standards are structured to guarantee consistency and regulate competence within professions. However, sometimes the means by which the Filipino educational system was measured was not fair. Filipino accountants, for example, fought for 20 years to be licensed in the United States based solely on the accreditation of their Filipino licenses. The rules for licensing certified public accountants state that foreign accountants can practice here without being recertified only if their native country's professional standards are equal to those of the United States. The Filipino accountants ultimately proved that though they lagged behind U.S. educational standards, they were nevertheless better educated than accountants from other countries who were allowed to practice in the United States without recertification.

Yet Filipinos faced professional discrimination on other levels as well. Many Filipino doctors found that their American colleagues did not want to work with foreigners; this sort of discrimination was especially hard to bear because the immigrant doctors had been welcomed first by the terms of the McCarran-Walter Act and by the Foreign Exchange Visitor Program. Their skills were desperately needed one year, then rejected another.

In the 1970s, Congress passed the Health Professions Educational Assistance Act, designed specifically to limit the immigration of East Indian and Filipino doctors (by 1969, India and the Philippines had surpassed Europe in providing scientists, engineers, and doctors to the United States; the Philippines was the main source of foreign-born physicians). The new act required that foreign doctors be further educated in the United States before being allowed to take licensing exams here. It also stipulated that these physicians must have a working knowledge of English and medical training comparable to American training.

These requirements were important in keeping U.S. standards high, but they also severely limited the Filipino doctors' ability to find positions worthy of their educational background. Because the wait to be licensed in the United States had suddenly been extended, many highly qualified professionals were required to take jobs beneath their training simply in order to make ends meet.

Some became technicians and lab workers in the hospitals in which they hoped to eventually work as doctors, while others were not as fortunate in finding jobs even vaguely related to their field. Many worked as clerks or cabdrivers just to make enough money to support their families, and didn't reveal their actual professions at job interviews for fear of being turned away as overqualified. One Filipino physician with 16 years' experience said he got his job as a meat cutter because his employers were impressed with how well he removed the meat from the bone!

The largest professional export from the Philippines since World War II has been nurses. There are currently 70,000 Filipina

nurses in the United States. But nursing *teachers* are now emigrating as well as their former students, so the quality of nursing education in the Philippines is declining. Currently, only half of Philippine nursing graduates pass their licensing exams. The Philippines is trying desperately to remedy this situation by training nurses more in community medicine (public and preventive medicine) and less in Western institutional medicine, hoping that this will keep the nurses in the Philippines. The government is also considering a requirement that nurses practice in the Philippines for two years before going abroad.

A Filipino-American chief pharmacist in San Francisco. Many Filipino medical professionals emigrated into the United States during shortages in the 1950s and 1960s.

Filipina nurses who emigrate face their own challenges in the United States. There are so many Filipina nurses in American hospitals that Tagalog is commonly spoken among the staff, but often this leads to conflict between the Filipinos and the nurses who do not speak Tagalog. Some hospitals have instituted "English only" rules to prohibit nurses from speaking foreign languages, including Tagalog, while on duty. Filipino nurses have protested that this is a violation of their constitutional right to free speech, and have filed lawsuits against these hospitals.

Farm and Factory Workers

For blue-collar Filipino workers who arrived here before the war, job progress was slow. They could not get jobs in factories until they were recruited to work for the defense industry in 1942. Even then, they were not allowed in the factory unions until after the war. Without union membership, many jobs were not open to them.

Farm workers were even slower to unionize. In the 1960s, Filipino farm workers led by Lary Dulay Itliong formed the Agricultural Workers Organizing Committee, which in 1965 struck against the California grape growers and, when it merged with the Mexican American National Farm Workers Association, led by Cesar Chavez, successfully won concessions from employers. The new union, known as the United Farm Workers Union, led one of the most famous and well-supported strikes in farm history.

Yet these workers still face hardship and prejudice. Many live in areas that have disintegrated into slums, and they cannot afford to move out. Many are supported only by Social Security, and their children and grandchildren have been unable to escape poverty. Some poor urban Filipino youths join gangs, which fight for dominance with Mexican, Chinese, and Vietnamese gangs.

The poorer farm and factory workers also face scorn from the newer Filipino immigrants, upper-middle-class professionals who look down upon the "old-timers." The newer immigrants, in turn, are considered by the older immigrants to be snobs. At times, it seems that Filipino immigrants are so diverse that no group of them escapes from prejudice, whether it be from without *or* within.

Power and Assimilation as Americans

Though Filipino Americans face many prejudices, they are not without power in the United States. They exert a great influence over American policies having to do with the Philippines, especially since Filipino Americans, as a group, have a lot of money to spend in politics. Pressure from lobbyists representing Filipino Americans convinced President Ronald Reagan to support legislation granting millions of dollars in aid to the Philippines. And financial support in 1986 from wealthy Filipino Americans helped overthrow Ferdinand Marcos's regime. So many Filipinos live abroad, in fact, that the Philippines National Assembly elects two representatives each year to represent Filipino expatriates.

Filipino Americans face cultural as well as political quandaries when they encounter American society. Because of the close association between the United States and the Philippines in

Former President
Ronald Reagan
looks on as
former President
Corazon Aquino
speaks at the
White House in
1986. Lobbying
by Filipino
Americans helped
convince Reagan
to support millions
of dollars of aid to
the Philippines.

the past century, Filipino Americans are quite accustomed to our society and its customs, and have, over the years, copied American fashions, music, and fads. Cultural exchange is certainly helped along by Filipinos' fluency in English. Less than 1 percent of Filipino Americans speak no English at all—few immigrant groups can boast such statistics.

Yet Filipino Americans still have some difficulties fitting in. Certainly, adjusting to our colder winters can be a challenge for people who were brought up very close to the equator, in a country that is generally hot and humid. American slang can pose another problem. New English words and phrases do not make their way as quickly to the Philippines as they do to more commercial countries like Japan, so Filipino immigrants may not understand a large part of modern American speech. For younger Filipino Americans, this can be particularly stressful in school, where native-born students are apt to be intolerant.

Also, younger Filipinos' typical fluency in English may disguise educational difficulties. Teachers who look for difficulty in English as a sign that the immigrant child needs extra help may be fooled by the ease with which Filipinos speak English. Their ability to converse, though, is not necessarily a sign that their prior education in the Philippines had been equal to American standards.

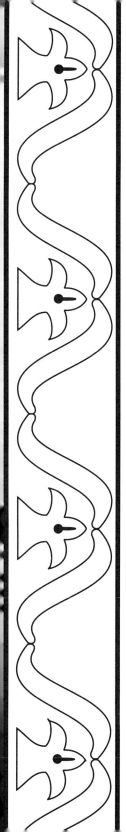

Maria Aviado
Typecasting

Maria Aviado is 25 years old. She is an actress living in Los Angeles, California. Her parents emigrated from the Philippines in 1965.

I grew up in California, and I wouldn't say that I felt prejudice when I was a kid. I went to a school with Mexicans, Southeast Asians, you name it. We were all just kids together. I didn't have one Filipino friend, just some cousins I would see on family occasions.

I was in the drama club in high school. I played Eliza in *My Fair Lady* and Emily in *Our Town*. No role was ever closed to me because I was a Filipina. It was the same in college, too, at UCLA. I got plenty of leads, and I got used to thinking I could do whatever I wanted.

Now I'm in the real world, and I'm finding new obstacles. I get some theater work in the Los Angeles area, and I want the chance to act in movies, too. But it seems that Asian women get pigeonholed. I'm young, so they want to stick me in a bathing suit and hang me on an evil drug dealer's arm. Or if there's a manipulative, cold-hearted "dragon lady" in a script, my agent will get a call. There's no in-between. If there's a role for a gutsy, intelligent woman, I'm not even considered. And comedy? Forget it. Although I've played everything from Molière to Neil Simon, casting agents tell me an Asian woman can't do comedy.

So one day it just hit me—I'm not considered because I'm not considered *American*. I grew up in L.A. I like cheeseburgers, apple pie, and Mustang convert-

ibles, just like anybody. But now I'm considered *exotic*.

Because of my name, Maria Aviado, sometimes casting directors will call because they think I'm Hispanic. I go to the casting call anyway, because I figure maybe it won't make a difference. And you know what? It always does. People will say, I'm sorry, we're looking for a Hispanic actress for this role. And I'll say, Why? And I don't get a good reason. Because she's sexy? Because she's hot-tempered? Filipinas don't have tempers?

I'll probably get the label of "difficult," which my friends tell me is the kiss of death. Funny, too. I'm "difficult" and I haven't even been on a movie set! I'm difficult because I say, Hey, not all Americans are blond, fellas! Open your eyes. I can play anything. Open your minds.

≡ **5** ≡

Life-styles

The Early Immigrants

The earliest Filipino Americans were restricted from associating with native-born Americans because of prejudice. They did gather as Filipinos, in pool halls, gambling houses, and dance halls, even in barbershops. Many of the early Filipino immigrants became barbers here because men in the Philippines freely cut one another's hair, and because so many Filipino immigrants were denied service in American barbershops. Barbershops were easy to establish in the 1910s and 1920s because a license was not needed to operate one. Filipino men gathered at these Filipino-run shops and there they told stories and jokes and enjoyed one another's company.

Filipinos were usually hired in groups to work on farms in those days, so they devised a way, as a group, of making the most of their wages. They developed the *encloso* system, in which all the Filipino workers on a farm pooled their earnings and shared the responsibilities of a single residence. Usually, the members of a group spoke a common dialect or were from the same island in the Philippines. By establishing a type of commune, these laborers became more independent of the farm owners while encouraging one another to work hard and earn money. The *encloso* system expanded on the Philippine tradition of mutual assistance, especially in times of need, and created places where Filipino culture could be maintained and shared. The system also created a sub- stitute family for men who were forced to live as bachelors while their wives and families remained in the Philippines.

Filipino students established similar life-styles in the cities. Because many of them had difficulty supporting themselves while in school, they lived three or four together in one apartment. Often, one or two of the residents worked while the others went to school. Sometimes the working Filipinos were not students at all but just hospitable friends. These men believed that someday the favor would be repaid.

Politics

Back when Filipino schoolboys and laborers pooled their resources simply to survive in the United States, their participation in politics was fairly limited. Though they might have been interested in what was going on back in the Philippines, they had neither the money nor the time to do anything about it. Only an elite few ever returned home to hold political office or to have any influence in Philippine politics. And in this country, Filipinos were barred from voting because they were not citizens. They were also excluded from the political process by prejudice and discrimination.

Today, however, Filipino Americans are quite involved in both American and Philippine politics, though they stand divided over current politics in the Philippines. There are both supporters of

(continued on page 89)

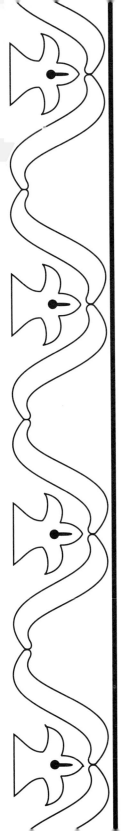

Manuel Joya
The Filipino Way

Manuel Joya is 81 years old. He lives with his son and daughter-in-law
in Los Angeles.

My family mortgaged everything they owned to send me to study in the United States. My godfather also contributed. I had many people back home believing in me. That's what made it so hard in the beginning. I almost starved, but there was no way I could give up and go back. I had to keep going forward.

I lived with four other Filipinos in a tiny apartment in Los Angeles. Some of us worked as busboys in restaurants, others as janitors. I worked part-time and went to school along with Fernando, my best friend. We paid less than the others for rent and food, since we were going to school. The rest of our roommates were glad to chip in extra. That was the way it worked then. And Fernando and I did eventually pay everyone back. Not only that, but I ended up marrying my roommate Virgilio's sister! I'm not sure if he considered that payback or not.

But back then, I couldn't see the future. Everything seemed black. I could barely manage to stay in school. Sometimes I was very discouraged. And then I'd look around and think, So what if I do graduate from college? What am I going to be, a janitor? A dishwasher?

One of my roommates who had been working as a houseboy was going to Chicago to live with a relative. He offered to introduce me to his employer, who would need a new houseboy. The job paid well, and it was better than working in a restaurant or a factory. But if I accepted the position, I would have to leave school.

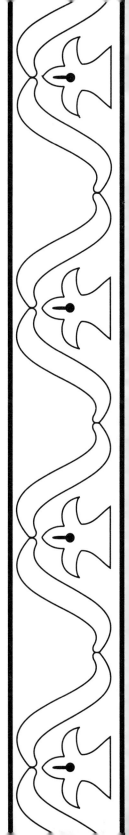

It was a tough decision, but I took the job.

I ended up living with this family for five years, until the war started. What a time! The man was an executive in a movie studio. He gave big parties every weekend. At Christmas, they would put a twenty-foot tree in the front hall, and underneath would be presents for big movie stars like Gary Cooper and Marlene Dietrich.

But for me, the glamor wore off. I had no personal life, and I worked from seven in the morning until midnight, or later. I think my employers liked me, but they didn't seem to think I would want to get married or have friends or finish college. I became friends with the cook, Carmelita, and her husband Antonio, the gardener. That was it. I hardly saw my old friends at all. On my afternoon off, somehow my boss would always have "just a few errands" for me to do. After a while, let me tell you, I was tired of this job. I hadn't left the Philippines to become a servant.

But I had pride, too, and I did my job well. I was able to save and pay back my roommates, add a little extra to help them, even send money back home to the Philippines. My parents considered me a success. But it really bothered me that I hadn't finished my education. In my eyes, I was a failure.

Then the war came. When I told my employers I was going to enlist— what a scene! They were so angry. Why should I join the war? they asked. I wasn't even American! Even when I pointed out politely that the Japanese had occupied my country, they still didn't get it.

I became a soldier, and I saw plenty of action in the Pacific. I was in many of the big battles, and it's a miracle I'm here talking to you today. I think that one thing that saved me was getting malaria right before Iwo Jima. I was too sick to go.

I went to college after the war, on the GI Bill. I majored in history, and I became a high-school teacher. I married my old roommate's sister, Pearl. We just ran into each other on the street one day, can you believe that? She was a beautiful lady, a nurse. She died five years ago.

When I think back on my early days, I think mostly of living with my friends, all sleeping in the same room, all helping each other. That's the Filipino way, you know. *Utang-na-loob.* [Debt of gratitude.] Young people today don't respect this. It's because they don't know how to trust.

Marcos and supporters of Aquino and Ramos living in the United States. When Ferdinand Marcos was exiled from the Philippines in 1986 and came to Hawaii, many of his followers cheered him upon his arrival. When he died in 1989, many Filipino Americans mourned for him and protested Corazon Aquino's decision not to allow his body into the Philippines for burial. When Marcos's wife, Imelda, faced charges of criminal racketeering for misdeeds committed during the years the Marcoses were in power, scores of Filipino Americans gathered on the steps of the New York City courthouse, in which her trial was being conducted, to show their love and support. When Imelda Marcos finally was allowed to return to the Philippines with her husband's remains, and when she decided to run for president in the 1992 election, she did so with the political and financial backing of Filipino Americans.

Some other Filipino Americans, though, were opposed to the U.S. government's decision to allow Ferdinand and Imelda Marcos to go to Hawaii. They felt that the United States should not grant favors to a man many Filipinos considered to be a corrupt politician, a murderer, and a torturer. Instead, they argued, this country should have protested his actions when he was still in power and refused his entrance into the United States after he was deposed. However, the United States' long-standing support of Marcos led President Ronald Reagan to decide in favor of the Marcoses' immigration.

Still other Filipino Americans opposed both Marcos *and* Aquino. They had fled Marcos's reign of terror but later found that human-rights violations continued under Corazon Aquino. Many Filipino human-rights lawyers protested Aquino's government from their self-imposed exile in the United States.

Education and Achievement

Filipino Americans have the power to influence politics today because, often, they're wealthy. After ten years in this country, the average Filipino-American family has a higher yearly income than the average white American family. Only Japanese Americans and East-Indian Americans are more successful. Of course, in a Filipino-American family, usually both the husband and wife work, and the term "family" as applied to Filipinos might describe a larger, extended clan than the typical white American nuclear family. In the United States, moreover, the Filipino-American unemployment rate is lower than the national average.

It is interesting to note, though, that studies show that compared with other Asian Americans, a second-generation Filipino American is less likely to earn more with each extra year of education beyond high school. This may imply that some of the discipline and status consciousness for which Filipinos are noted is lost in a single generation in this country. (Or the figures could be misleading, as most present-day second-generation Filipino Americans are the children of agricultural and other blue-collar workers. The children of the status-conscious professionals who arrived in the 1960s and later are only now entering the work force.) Nevertheless, Filipino Americans still hold education and professional achievement in high regard. The reverence for education instilled in the Philippines during the U.S. colonial era has never left the Filipino people, and they carry it with them when they emigrate to America.

Despite their relative anonymity as an ethnic group, Filipino Americans have managed to influence the education system in

Imelda Marcos entering U.S. federal court in 1988 to be arraigned on racketeering charges for the years her husband ruled the Philippines. Many Filipino Americans rallied to her support during the trial.

areas where large numbers of them live. In California, where Filipinos are the largest Asian ethnic group, some schools teach Filipino-American children in both English and Tagalog.

Social Organizations

One of the ways Filipino Americans attempt to exert influence as a group is by pooling their resources and forming social organizations. Since the first Manilamen of Louisiana formed the *Sociedad de Beneficincia de los Hispano Filipinas de Nueva Orleans* in 1870, Filipinos have gathered together in societies.

In Hawaii, the sugar-plantation workers and their descendants have been forming hometown associations since the first immigrants arrived, bringing together residents of the same Philippine town or speakers of a common dialect. These associations, originally established to provide aid to their members who had no health benefits or retirement funds, give money to members who are ill or to the families of members who die, and they often pay for funerals. They also send money back to the Philippines to be used for the benefit of the towns from which they come. Sometimes they establish scholarship funds or build hospitals or schools. The greater buying power of the U.S. dollar makes this practice very successful.

Filipino Americans also come together to form beneficial societies dedicated to preserving Philippine culture and establishing a place where Filipinos can find comfort and assistance from their fellow citizens. There are more of these societies on the West Coast than on the East Coast, primarily because most of the Filipinos in the East are professionals with moderate to high

incomes who may not need aid in assimilating to the culture around them. (Generally, it seems that Filipino Americans outside these societies are less inclined to offer assistance to their fellow countrymen than the Filipino Americans of the 1920s and 1930s did.)

Their organizations give Filipino Americans an opportunity to achieve positions of power to which they might not otherwise have access in American society. To that end, the politics of the Filipino-American associations has become rather competitive and has come to resemble the fierce political battling of the Philippines. Those running for office in the associations have been known to be ruthless in their campaign tactics, mortgaging their homes to buy votes and sabotaging the campaigns of their opponents.

The editor of Seattle's *Filipino American Bulletin*, a successful Filipino-American publication. Many similar newspapers are short-lived, owing to the lack of national support.

Ironically, the stated goals of the Filipino organizations are not political at all. These are meant to be social organizations, providing Filipino Americans with a sense of belonging. They sponsor dances, contests, scholarships, and trips to the Philippines. In addition, the societies are watchdogs of racial equality. The myriad newspapers operated by Filipino Americans report on anti-Filipino sentiment and incidents. Unfortunately, most of these newspapers are short-lived local enterprises with little power or influence over the Filipino-American community at large.

Like the newspapers, the societies are local endeavors. No national Filipino-American organization exists, though some of the California groups have become large (up to 4,000 members) and relatively powerful. Attempts to unify the groups nationally have been fruitless so far. The associations have difficulty unifying partly because of differing opinions on the political situation in the Philippines and partly because the Filipino people speak so many different languages. The first thing two Filipino people usually do upon meeting is to identify themselves by the regions from which they come and the languages that they speak. In the Philippines, two communities only 50 miles apart may speak two totally different dialects. Trying to unify such a diverse culture into one influential body has been a difficult task for Filipino Americans.

Religion

Filipino Americans do often experience unity, though, in their religious beliefs. The majority of the Filipino immigrants to the United States are Roman Catholic, and they bring this faith with

them to their new home. Filipino Americans were not always welcome in the Catholic churches of the United States, however. The
first Filipino immigrants were denied the sacraments, such as
Communion, baptism, and marriage, in many Catholic parishes
along the West Coast. Often, a congregation felt "threatened" by a
large group of Filipino men attending services.

It took some time before the Filipinos established their own
churches. Throughout the early wave of Filipino immigration to
this country, Catholicism often was left by the wayside. Because
women are typically the guardians of the faith, many Filipino-
American men neglected their religious duties until Filipinas
began immigrating here. When Filipinas arrived in great numbers
after World War II, Filipino churches began to be established with
greater frequency.

The traditions associated with Catholicism are an integral
part of Filipino-American life. Christenings, confirmations, wed-
dings, and anniversaries are all celebrated with lavish parties.

A christening is an important event in a Filipino's life
because it is the time the godparent is chosen. Godparents are
as important in a Filipino family as actual parents, because a
godparent is responsible for much of the child's upbringing. In
the Philippines, godparents are chosen for their ability to provide
for a child should something happen to the parents. Often these
godparents are not close friends of the family but are respected
members of the community. Not only are the godparents responsible for ensuring the religious education of the Filipino child,
but they often pay for a child's secular education as well.
Becoming godparents in the Philippines is almost like marrying
into a family; godparents occasionally move in with the parents
of their godchild.

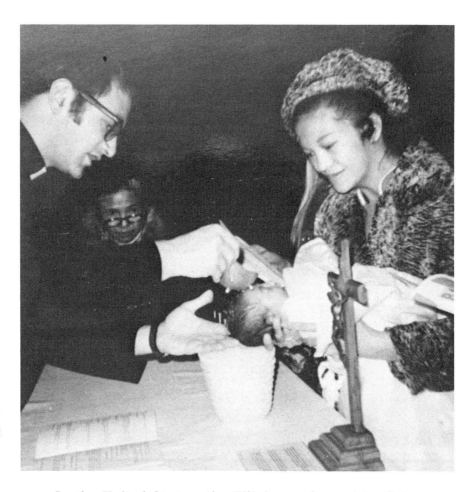

A Filipino-American godmother participates in the rite of baptism. Godparents are considered a very important part of Filipino life.

In the United States, the Filipino godparent tradition survives, but it is not always as important. The extended Filipino family shrinks in America, and the godparents play a smaller role in raising and educating the children. However, the social and political connections that godparents are able to exploit on behalf of their godchildren are still a determining force when parents choose these surrogate guardians.

Filipino-American Protestants are not as fixed in tradition

as the Roman Catholics, perhaps because Protestantism was introduced into the Philippines only at the turn of the 20th century. The American colonialists brought with them their own missionaries and established churches that a few Filipinos joined. Many of these newly converted Protestants benefited as the recipients of scholarships to study in the United States, where they also found that their faith opened doors for them in education through such organizations as the Young Men's Christian Association (YMCA). Other Filipino Americans became Protestants when they had difficulty finding Catholic parishes that would let them attend Mass.

Filipino-American Culture

Filipinos have traveled to this country carrying with them the arts of their homeland. From food to dance to music to painting to literature, Filipinos have distinguished themselves as notable ethnic artists. In addition, Filipino Americans have established new traditions in the arts, combining historic Philippine crafts with new American influences.

Philippine food, a unique combination of Spanish, American, and native flavors, epitomizes this cultural merging. It has recently become a popular ethnic cuisine in America, especially along the West Coast. Serving such entrées as steak or fried chicken alongside *paella*, a Spanish dish, and *bagoong*, a Philippine shrimp dish, Filipino restaurants provide a wide range of offerings. Though they have served in the past largely as places where Filipino Americans could get authentic Philippine food, these restaurants increasingly attract non-Filipino customers as well.

Filipino Americans re-creating a traditional Muslim wedding dance. Philippine dance traditions are celebrated by Filipino-American troupes.

Similarly, Filipino-American influences and styles have emerged recently in the visual arts and in dance. Filipino artists living in America have impressed critics with pieces depicting the experience of the first Filipino immigrants. The paintings and sculptures often pay tribute to the old-timers, drawing attention to the hard work they performed and the racial prejudices they endured. Other Filipino-American artists have created political art that would have been banned in the Philippines during the Marcos regime. These artists' works evoke images of the fear and defi- ance inspired by Marcos's rule.

The formation of ethnic dance troupes has given rise to a recent revival of interest in the traditional Filipino dances dating back to the Spanish colonial days and earlier. When the Spanish conquered the Philippines, many dance traditions were lost. However, the Spanish admired enough of the Philippine dances to preserve them and blend them with Spanish dances like the *fandango*. Filipino Americans, wishing to see Philippine dances included in international exhibitions, have started companies to bring traditional ethnic dances to the American public.

Filipino-American writers have also brought their art to the American public through autobiographical books describing the hardships of the immigrant life. Two such narratives are the previously mentioned Manuel Buaken's critically acclaimed *I Have Lived with the American People*, written during the 1940s, which gives an inspiring description of Buaken's journey from scholar to dishwasher to schoolboy to noted author and lecturer, and Carlos Bulosan's *America Is in the Heart: A Personal History*, written in the 1970s, the product of Bulosan's years as a writer, poet, and labor organizer.

Traditions and Values

The autobiographies written by Buaken and Bulosan illustrate the strong Filipino spirit and dedication to traditions and values, which managed to survive more than 300 years of oppressive Spanish rule. These values have made their way into the Filipino-American life-style.

The Filipino attitude toward women is distinctly liberal. Before the Spanish arrived, Filipino tribal women were considered absolute equals to men. They had the right to hold property, and they kept their maiden names when they married. They also had equal say in all family decisions. Though Spanish rule was oppressive and sexist, the belief in the equality of the sexes survived. Even now, though the husband in a Filipino family is often considered the decision maker of the family, the wife controls the family finances without challenge.

Currently, the Philippines continues to promote equality between men and women. Little discrimination exists against women in the workplace. Women are equal to men in many fields, including medicine (half the physicians and a majority of the optometrists, dentists, and pharmacists in the country are women). Women have been represented on the Philippine Supreme Court since 1930, and most Filipinas are better educated then Filipino men. According to Philippine law, day-care must be available to all working parents, and most jobs offer maternity and paternity leave.

These attitudes toward women's rights have found their way into the Filipino-American life-style, where women, single or married, are as likely to work as men. However, the day-care and maternity-leave systems available in the Philippines are not as common in the United States. Perhaps this is one reason that Filipino-American families tend to be smaller then native Filipino families. Filipinas in this country have fewer children on average than their counterparts in the Philippines

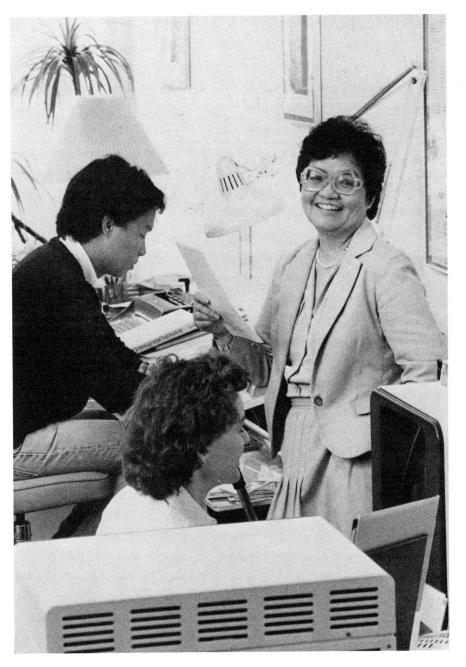

The owner of a
marketing com-
munications and
public relations
firm—one of the
many Filipino-
American women
who works outside
the home. In the
Philippines,
women and men
are considered
equals and
programs to
support women
who work are
often mandatory.

or even than native-born American women.

The Filipino-American family is also smaller than the native Filipino family because the customary extended family of the Philippines is less common here. Many members of the extended family may be left behind when Filipinos emigrate to the United States, and Filipino Americans often consider this a disadvantage to raising children. The extended family plays a vital role in preserving values by helping to maintain discipline in the family. The authority of many adult relatives can be a very effective tool when raising a defiant child. Still, many Filipino–American parents feel that the benefits of raising their children in the United States offset any disadvantages caused by the lack of an extended family system.

In general, the importance of the family in Filipino life does not lessen in the United States. The family, rather than the individual, is considered the center of Filipino existence. This is perhaps one of the reasons Filipino Americans are less likely than other Americans to divorce. Family tradition discourages divorce, which is still illegal in the Philippines.

Filipinos believe that one owes much to the family, especially to one's parents. In the Philippines, there is a tradition of *utang-na-loob*, or "debt of gratitude," a debt that must be paid back. Whether it is a favor granted by a friend or the years of sacrifice a parent gives for a child, the recipient of goodwill owes the giver a favor in return. The debt is considered strong and important and cannot be paid back merely with money. Much of the favoritism that was practiced by President Marcos stems from this system, and it still prevails among Filipino politicians. *Utang-na-loob* led early Filipino Americans to help one another through times of need. The charitable friend is always guaranteed goodwill in return.

Another common Filipino expression that Filipino Americans preserve is "*bahala-na*." It means "come what may," and it is invoked when Filipinos try to justify why things happen the way they happen. "*Bahala-na*" expresses an acceptance of fate, and it may help explain why Filipino agricultural workers seldom acted against their horrible working conditions in the 1920s and 1930s or against the swindlers who cheated them out of so much during this time.

Holiday Celebrations

Three major holidays are celebrated with great enthusiasm in the Philippines, and Filipino Americans have brought these celebrations to America. Two are uniquely Filipino interpretations of Christian holidays and the third is a glorious commemoration of a great Filipino hero.

The month surrounding Christmas is one grand party in the Philippines. The festivities start on December 16, with a morning Mass. Each night thereafter, Filipinos gather to sing carols. On Christmas Eve, the different villages and communities compete to see who has built the biggest *parol*, a large lantern that serves as the Philippine equivalent of a Christmas tree. Then the Filipinos begin the *Panunulayan*, a procession much like a Christmas pageant. Actors portraying Mary and Joseph lead the parade and ask nine times at homes for shelter. Each time, they are turned away, until the final time, when they ask at the church. Afterward, the parish celebrates the midnight Mass, called *Misa de Gallo*.

(continued on page 106)

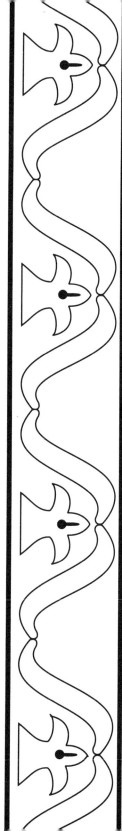

April Chabet
Fiesta

April Chabet is a doctor living in Philadelphia. She was born and educated in the Philippines but completed her medical training in the United States.

I studied nursing in the Philippines, but I quit after a year and decided to become a doctor. It made more sense to me. I wanted to be in charge of things. When I first came to the United States, I had to work as a medical technician until I was able to complete my training and get certified in Pennsylvania. That was hard, since I had already been a doctor in the Philippines. But now I have my own practice as an obstetrician.

My little sister will be eighteen this year, and she's talking about coming to the United States. My parents want her to live with me and go to a college nearby. They think I can keep an eye on her. Well, I'll do my best, but I don't think my parents realize that I'm rarely home. I have a thriving practice, and babies take time. If you ask me what color my kitchen appliances are, I honestly don't think I could tell you.

Being a Filipino American is, to me, like being in limbo. I can't go to some "Filipinotown" in Philadelphia and immerse myself in culture if I get homesick. There's no concentrated area for Filipinos, no sense of our culture. I have to rely on letters from home, and pictures, and the sounds of Tagalog from the nurses I hear as I walk the halls in the hospital.

One thing I miss in the United States is an extended family that looks out

r each other. That, and some sort of day-care. I look at the women who are hav-
g babies and I wonder, How will they manage? They need to work, but any care
r babies eats up a salary. Very few fathers get family leave. Women have it
arder here. There's no doubt about it.

My sister wants to study public health policy. She is intelligent and curious
nd has so much energy, I have a feeling she'll exhaust me. I'll enjoy it. I'm look-
g forward to having her here, a little piece of home. I'm already thinking of how
uch fun Christmas will be. Americans don't have a *fiesta* season here like there is
home—there we don't stop after the twelve days of Christmas, we keep on cele-
rating for a further ten whole days! When my sister comes, we'll just have to stir
p a little Filipino culture on our own.

✳   ✳   ✳

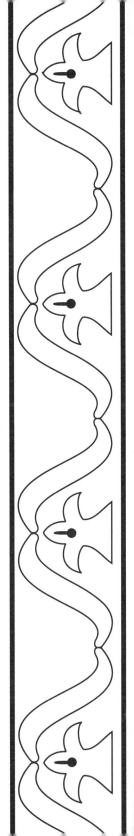

After Christmas, the celebration continues. On January 6 (the Feast of the Epiphany), the ten-day fiesta season begins. The focus of the *fiesta* is the charity and goodwill Jesus preached. Daily Masses continue for the ten days, ending with the Feast of El Niño, when the image of the Christ child is brought to the church.

During Easter season, the celebrations are almost as elaborate as those at Christmas. The week before Easter is known as *Sinakulo*, when the life, death, and Resurrection of Christ are reenacted. After Easter Day, during *Salubong,* Filipinos re-create the meeting of Christ and Mary at the Resurrection.

Each of these traditions was introduced by the Spanish during their colonial years to interest the Filipinos in Catholicism. Yet they appeal to much older Filipino traditions of ritual reenactment. These elaborate celebrations are often re-created in the United States by Filipino-American Catholics.

In spite of the high place of religious holidays in the life of Filipinos, though, the most honored holiday of the Philippine year is *Rizal Day*, named for José Protasio Rizal, a Philippine national hero. Trained in Spain as a doctor, Rizal was also an author, poet, botanist, and scientist who spoke five languages. In the 19th century, he fought against Spanish rule and for Philippine independence and in 1886 wrote a powerful book called *Noli me tangere* (*Touch Me Not*), depicting the plight of the Filipinos under the Spanish. He was exiled by the Spanish for having written this book, but continued to write, anyway. He wrote *El filibusterismo* (*Filibustering*) in 1891 to call attention to the inequalities of Spanish rule.

In 1892, Rizal returned to the Philippines but was confirmed

by the Spanish to the island of Mindanao. However, he continued to fight their oppressive rule from his new home. At the same time, he continued his studies in the jungle, discovering new plant and animal species, engineering water systems, building schools for the local natives, translating books, and teaching people to read.

By 1896, a revolt against Spanish rule had begun among the Filipinos, and Rizal, as its leader, was brought to trial by the Spanish without representation. On December 30, 1896, he was executed by a firing squad. That day is still commemorated among Filipinos worldwide as Rizal Day. The festivities of Rizal Day rival American Fourth of July celebrations.

A *Pista Sa Nayon* celebration in Seattle, Washington. Filipino Americans celebrate many traditional Philippine holidays.

Rizal epitomizes the spirit of the Filipino people. Faced with many obstacles throughout their history, Filipinos have managed to preserve their traditions and create a place for themselves as one of the most educated peoples in the modern world. While events of the last half century have placed the prosperity of the Philippines in grave danger, forcing Filipinos to flee their native land and emigrate to the United States, as Filipino Americans they continue their commitment to education and achievement.

For Further Reading

Cordova, Fred. *Filipinos, Forgotten Asian Americans: A Pictorial Essay.* Dubuque, Iowa: Kendall/Hunt Publishing Co., 1983.

Stern, Jennifer. *The Filipino Americans.* New York: Chelsea House, 1989.

Vallangca, Caridad Concepcion. *The Second Wave: Pinay & Pinoy (1945-1960).* San Francisco: Strawberry Hill Press, 1987.

Vallangca, Roberto. *Pinoy, the First Wave.* San Francisco: Strawberry Hill Press, 1977.

Voices, a Filipino American Oral History. Stockton, Cal.: Filipino Oral History Project, 1984.

Index